Pierre Cardin

pierre cardin evolution
furniture and design
Benjamin Loyauté

Photography by Jérôme Faggiano and Nils Herrmann

Flammarion

ÉDITORIAL DIRECTION, FLAMMARION
COLLECTION STYLES AND DESIGN
Suzanne Tise-Isoré

EDITORIAL COORDINATION, PIERRE CARDIN
Emmanuel Beffy

GRAPHIC DESIGN
Bernard Lagacé

TRANSLATED FROM THE FRENCH BY
Caractères et cætera

COPYEDITING
Jonathan Sly

EDITORIAL ASSISTANT
Delphine Montagne

PHOTOGRAPHY
Jérôme Faggiano and Nils Herrmann

COLOR SEPARATION
Les artisans du Regard, Paris

Distributed in North America by Rizzoli International
Publications, Inc.

Simultaneously published in French as *Pierre Cardin
Évolution, meubles et design*
© Flammarion, 2006
© Pierre Cardin, 2006

English-language edition
© Flammarion, 2006
© Pierre Cardin, 2006

06 07 08 3 2 1

Dépôt légal: 09/2006
FC0527-06-IX
ISBN-10: 2-0803-0527-1
ISBN-13: 9782080305275
Printed in Italy by Geca

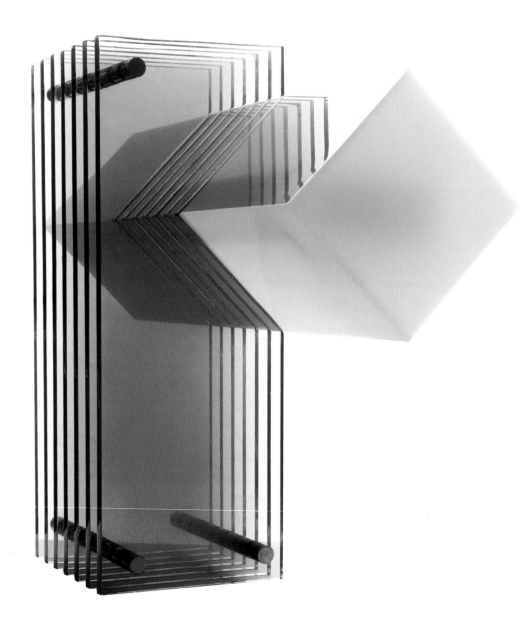

COVER Espace chair by François Cante-Pacos
in black lacquered wood with sculpted back,
1972 (see page 141).
ENDSHEETS Wallpaper design, Pierre Cardin's Design
Studio, 1970–75.
PRECEDING PAGE Pierre Cardin in front of one
of his sculptures, 1971.
RIGHT Cube lamp made of seven sheets of Plexiglas
connected by metal rods. The suspended cube
is cut in white Perspex, circa 1974 (see page 57).
PAGE 6 Pierre Cardin in front of a Francesco Bocola
lamp-sculpture situated on Marc Held's desk.
Photograph by Henri Cartier-Bresson, 1974.

Sommaire

Interview with Pierre Cardin
Benjamin Loyauté

You are a symbol of the 1970s, an era during which you were a creative traveler and empiricist. What do you recall most about this time?

When it came to materials, for creating objects, equipment or especially furniture, people had never really used "liquid matter". The 1970s succeeded in using liquids, like polyurethane, to make solid shapes that went in all directions. It was simply a question of following one's imagination. Unlike "square" wooden furniture, cut and shaped with a saw then assembled in a geometric pattern, we used all types of materials, such as foam and plastics, to make more organic shapes. The 1970s was one of the most creative periods. Imaginative minds were able to create furniture that matched their original ideas. For me, it was the first time shapes could be interpreted. So I let my imagination run wild with rubber, a material of liquid origin, derived from oil. My life is based on creation. I wanted to make furniture that was different. I like new ideas and my 1970s were the fruit of this.

How old were you when you designed your first piece of furniture?

When I was eight, I had a friend called Dumas whose father was called Samud—he had reversed the letters of his name. Dumas had a carpenter's bench and I'd go work with him, making furniture from leftover wood shavings and glue, and object-sculptures from small pieces of wood. The name Samud amused me.

As far back as 1968, you said "designing a dress or a piece of furniture shares the same dimension; furniture must live through the body". Would you agree that you were the first couturier of furniture?

The difference is that a dress has a life and has to move; furniture cannot. It is harder to make a dress than a piece of furniture; you imagine the line or feature of furniture then produce it. This isn't so easy with dresses. The approach is similar, though, I believe. Making sleeves for a dress and legs for a table aren't so different. The research into lines and materials is the same for both. Furniture is similar to couture, even though I find furniture easier to create. At the time, as today, there were no more hard, fast rules defining furniture. We could exploit all its possibilities, to create forms both eccentric and functional. This is what I tried to do: make furniture that wasn't dull. If it hadn't been me, someone else would have done it, but I felt the role suited me and I became attached to it. If I am a "couturier of furniture" it is perhaps because of the duality of my furniture; it can be read back and front, as "utilitarian sculpture". My dresses are living sculptures, so why shouldn't my furniture be sculpture too?

Your creations are strongly infused with notions of the infinite, of space and the future. You seem to have created furniture ranges for which you alone hold the key—can you explain to us your esthetic typology and mandalas, such as the sphere and the pyramid?

I don't think there is any mystery to them. They are shapes created with a pencil that I adapted to furniture. They obviously include much symbolism that is not necessarily my own. Generally speaking, I have always liked round shapes, which for me are infinite; they have no end, like a globe, or anything that rolls; these represent the infinite. I think my Roulette pants and the NASA modules greatly influenced my direction like many other designers. My furniture is the opposite of straight, sober, clean lines; it is furniture made up of organic cells; all I did was reveal their esthetic quality.

Through this common quest for a new esthetic, what was your relationship to the great designers of the 1970s, like Joe Colombo?

I met Joe Colombo at the Milan Triennale. Francesco Bocola knew him well and introduced us. You know when you buy a work of art, it's good to meet the artist. The same applied to me, especially with Italian, then French designers. After many talks with Bocola, for example, we finally defined the television as an eye. So we made one. Our work together was unprecedented.

Your expert ability to appreciate the precision work of a craftsman gave you a feel for marquetry, precious woods, and working with lacquer, but didn't stop you using more innovative materials. Could a combination of both approaches be said to be a benchmark of avant-garde quality?

It's an idea that has a certain relevance. For example I thought that rubber and metal might work well together, like wood and new generation lacquers. Quality can only come through precision, a word used by cabinetmakers and new technologists alike. I'm no jack-of-all-trades. When you touch on an area, you have to deepen your knowledge of it.

In the 1960s and 1970s, the "smooth" esthetic was a synonym for speed and purity. Do you think you were the first to officially bring about a more hedonistic rapport with the body through your creations?

I worked like a sculptor; in fact if you put miniature replicas of my work on a table, they can be compared to sculptures. There is a sensuality, a carnal aspect to my furniture that lacquer tinges with Asian culture. Lacquer is like skin that you want to touch. Furniture design has always been influenced by architects and sculptors. I wanted to make furniture like sculpture, to look at from all angles, like the bodies that I clothe.

CLOCKWISE Wool-velour overcoat with a leather belt, autumn-winter collection, 1962; Red woolen tailored overcoat with broad asymmetrical scarf, autumn-winter collection, 1963; Pleated silk cocktail dress, spring summer collection 1963; Long black silk crepe sheath dress with a white gazar cape, spring summer collection 1961; Red woolen overcoat, autumn-winter collection 1954.
FACING PAGE White woolen overcoat with fox fur trim, Hublot hat, autumn-winter collection 1966.

FACING PAGE Fitting session, the creation of a canvas three-dimensional model, 1970. CLOCKWISE Vinyl necklace and glasses, autumn-winter collection 1970; Sculptured woolen dress, autumn-winter collection 1971; Glasses, autumn-winter collection 1970; Cascade necklace with a jersey outfit, autumn-winter collection 1970.

In the early 1980s, you made furniture prototypes from fabric, a kind of conclusion to your work. Could it be said that at that moment your cycle was complete?

I remember them; they were made of wire covered in white jersey. I was inspired by the artist Christo, who wrapped up bridges. I chose to wrap up a sculpture and make it utilitarian. The last items of furniture we made were shelves that I wanted to put in our shop windows. That meant I had to work on the three dimensions, like with my dresses.

As a visionary, going where others would never dare to venture, you had no trouble switching from unique pieces to large series. What is your fondest memory of this mass production to which all designers today aspire?

For me, it was the present, it wasn't visionary. I think all designers should be visionaries. We started mass production with Italy. I had a whole team around me as I did for fashion designing. I am both an artist and an industrialist. You can sculpt a piece just as you can sculpt your approach over time. Nothing was impossible; we created and put our names to everything we could, as industrialists do: coffee makers, lamps, cars, planes, household linen, watches, kitchens, and more. Mass production enabled us to tackle design and furniture destined for all homes. It was an adventure of which others can justifiably be jealous.

During the 1970s and 1980s at the *Espace,* you held a whole host of contemporary art exhibitions, as well as concerts and plays. Do you think that the crossover between music, fashion and design is necessary for innovation?

I'd set everything going at once: fashion, exhibitions, music, theater, furniture, they all worked together. Everything is dissociable and indissociable. My inspiration comes from architecture, but also from fashion and music. This is what makes me a creator. I also created spectacles, cufflinks, ties, shoes, and pants. I can go to bed in Cardin beds, sit in Cardin armchairs, eat in Cardin dining rooms, light my house, go to the theater or an exhibition, and never leave my empire. All these sometimes entirely unconnected things are nevertheless signed by Pierre Cardin. You've got to know how to look around you.

How would you define yourself today? As an artist, a designer, or perhaps a company?

I would define myself as a sculptor.

Today, your designs and esthetic seem to have been adopted by a whole generation of designers. They all display influences from the Seventies in their approach. What is your perception of this?

However impossible it seems, I made roughly one hundred items of furniture in over ten years. People often talk about cycles, but you need to stay ahead to create fashion, not just revive 1970s trends. Unfortunately people are all too often fearful, making it easier for them to stay in their comfort zones than wear something that cannot be worn, or sit on something that has not yet been accepted as a chair. All creation makes people uncomfortable, the unknown makes people uncomfortable: it creates a projection into their own future. We criticize this, but we always end up taking it on board. Good taste has nothing to do with creation. You have to look far into the future to influence the public gaze. Maybe in ten, fifty or a hundred years, the most unwearable fashions and most unlikely furniture will have become accepted, or even obsolete. The 1970s have gained widespread acceptance, and become a sign of good taste. It only took twenty years for my furniture to become the center of attention. ∎

ABOVE Pierre Cardin's apartment in 1964. The globe stands
on a Louis XV desk located between the lounge and dining room.
We can also make out the embroidered, lacquered silk screen from
the Imperial Palace in Tokyo, and Maria Pergay's silver hen, key
elements in the birth of Pierre Cardin's interior design of the 1970s.
RIGHT Long dress in pale green duchess satin, 1971.

Pierre Cardin: Design for Living

Art and design have both been open to diversity and plays on form for twenty years and it is now acceptable to combine committed, partisan esthetics with daring, entertaining visions. Within this ecumenical perspective, Pierre Cardin has been a major innovator and provocateur. Early on, his work created a breach in the history of design that, until then, had set its modern purists against its "romantics", and even against its "adventurers" and the heretics of the "fine design" tradition. Today, the debate surrounding forms and functions, materials and surfaces has abated; the time has come to appreciate Pierre Cardin, the designer.

The banks of the Seine, Paris, 1964; the scene is set: a winter garden bedecked with plants and furniture, discreet lighting by evening, reminiscent of what Pierre Cardin himself calls "a décor from a Marcel Proust novel"; the ground floor of a vast Napoleon III building, culminating in a glasshouse and crammed with antiques: dark-toned Renaissance furniture and light, 18th-century pieces, renowned for their high quality. The overall effect is one that James Tissot might have painted.

Back in the 1950s, Cardin was already a man of daring when it came to mixing genres; he did not have to wait for Napoleon III styles to come back into fashion (which eventually happened in the late 1970s). He was already sensitive to the ideas of lesser-known icons such as Madeleine Castaing and recurring traces of her style can still be found in his home. He had met Charles de Beistegui in the company of Jean Cocteau and Christian Bérard, and had already acquired a taste for precision, grace and beauty from his own friends and those of Christian Dior, with whom he began his career in 1946. However, like the collector Jacques Doucet, who sold his 18th-century collection to concentrate on the avant-garde, Cardin had also started to focus on the art of his era; the stylist had turned patron of the arts and started preaching his own vision of futuristic fashions.

The change in his vital décor began with touches of Oriental and Middle Eastern art in his entrance hall; his smaller rooms filled with Asian Buddhas and objects from Mesopotamia. He enhanced his interior and its black marble floors with a pair of Japanese screens, a sumptuous symbol of Imperial Japan. The screens originated from the Imperial palace in Tokyo, and were a gift from Princess Takamatsu herself. Cardin had first visited Japan in 1957 and was besotted by the country. He made the screens a key feature of his epic interior design universe as early as 1968, interviewed in 1964, he explained: "They were central to the decoration of my whole apartment. I believe you should always start with an object or piece of furniture you love and build on it to create a décor that reflects your personality."

At this stage, his 1970s lyricism, the keynote to the worldwide success of his empire, was already visible in his choice of armchairs, with their bands of color, and a green, blue and yellow Chinese rug. In these days, a contemporary-styled bust of Adonis gazed upon a globe stood atop his desk, a singular expression of his desire for conquest already apparent when he created his Bubble dress in 1954. For Pierre Cardin, an inveterate worker, the world would never stop spinning. So busy was he trotting the globe of fashion that he could never have imagined he was writing the novel of his own life, a fable in which furniture turns into sculpture and design becomes king.

Thus the story begins in this Proustian apartment, the elements of the design saga already in place. Another example, the hieratic silver cockerel perched on his dining table, created by Maria Pergay. It was a time when well-to-do Parisians were replacing their Boulle dressers and Louis XVI chairs with classic Bauhaus. For Pierre Cardin, however, the future was already in the present day as, with gay abandon, he combined old and avant-garde Italian designs, another presage of things to come in 1970s when the deliberate mismatching of styles created a new feminine elegance, a 1940s—1960s blend.

The stylist had already revolutionized the field of fashion. His vivid dreams of the human body had brought about groundbreaking creations: thermoformed Cardine, Cosmocorps, Satellite hats, vinyl leathers, and lacquered Rodhia raincoats, each a celebration of a new vision, lauded by the international press. After the launch of a women's prêt-à-porter range in 1963, a masterstroke, Cardin's fashion house began to resemble a laboratory of dreams. From the imaginings to emerge from this period and their incompletion, Cardin was led to derive his own theory of fashion that he then applied to the bold domain of "environmental design", as American critics termed it. The Cardin brand now mastered its own destiny; the foundations for Cardin's total creative universe had been laid.

At the end of the Sixties, France experienced a cultural explosion. The 1968 upheavals were accompanied by their own cultural equivalents: structuralism had reconfigured philosophy, the *film d'auteur* had revolutionized cinema and, in literature, the *nouveau roman* had altered the very structure of narrative, challenging the conventions of the traditional novel. In tune with these changes, Cardin altered the composition of fashion and developed new ways of understanding it, just as Robert Venturi had led the postmodern reaction to functionalism with his 1966 work *Complexity and Contradiction in Architecture.*

In this era of mass housing, inspired by Le Corbusier, Cardin had already dabbled in architectural crossovers. He had designed futuristic uniforms for smiling, glacial nurses working in Jean Maneval's Bubble Houses. He also devised a hospital room in which white polyurethane furniture was combined with Charles Eames chairs,

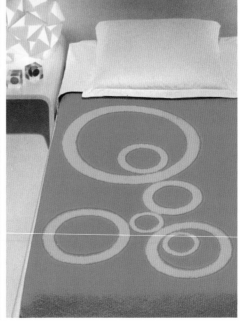

CLOCKWISE Models in futuristic nurse's uniforms, designed by Pierre Cardin, posing on the steps of one of Jean Maneval's Bubble houses. The 390-square-foot cells were transformed into hospitals by the couturier, circa 1969–70; Room in a hospital as designed by Pierre Cardin, circa 1969; Logo designed by Alain Carré for Pierre Cardin, circa 1970–71; Woolen cover designed by Cardin's Design Studio and produced by Toison d'or, circa 1975; Model posing at a desk with futurist lines in one of Jean Maneval's Bubble houses.

echoes of the staff medical center Dior included on the top floor of his Avenue Montaigne headquarters in the fifties, designed by Pierre Guariche, Serge Mouille and Mathieu Matégot. He had a dream of autocracy and autonomous worlds in which the fantasy of a self-enclosed society was underpinned by style in all its imperial glory, a desire that Pierre Cardin turned into reality. "Cardinisation" became the press's new buzzword, a word that already revealed the existence of an empire. For Cardin was, by now, a style in his own right, as famous as De Gaulle or Brigitte Bardot. For sportswomen, businessmen and pop-fuelled youngsters, he created whole ranges of consumer products from household linen to bicycles and furniture. Nothing escaped his touch; his name was branded everywhere. Life in Cardin became reality.

The nearest design history has ever come to its own Big Bang took place in 1969, the year that Gaetano Pesce, Ugo La Pietra, Archizoom and Superstudio published their manifestos. This group of anti-conformists claimed that imagination should hold a central place in design, and backed their case with an array of entertaining furniture at the Milan Triennale in 1968. The exhibition exposed the world to the excitement of Italian and Scandinavian creations. *Time* magazine, 23 December 1969, led with "Those Designing Europeans" and informed its readers that the design epicenter of the world was now in Western Europe. Italians were noted for their furniture and Germans their technology; a Frenchman, Pierre Cardin, was praised for his "environmental design". For the first time, department stores displayed inflatable furniture and psychedelic crockery in their windows and extolled the virtues of pasticcio, imitation leather, molded plastic and regular metal. Leatherette and bamboo prints covered walls, banks and offices to the extent that the elite of the design world was submerged in the new forms allowed by polyurethane. While Joe Colombo and Ettore Sottsass attempted to create different lifestyles from new objects and furniture, leading interior designers like Charles Sévigny for Hubert de Givenchy, and collectors like Roger Vivier, mixed the old and contemporary to produce "simplified" classical structures. In the ensuing esthetic mayhem, artists turned their hand to furniture.

It was in this prevailing creative climate that the review *Domus* announced the launch of Pierre Cardin's first design collection, the "Environment" collection of 1968–69. It included Venini vases by the architect Ludovico Diaz de Santillana, and a range of desk accessories for ladies and businessmen. The collection also represented small-scale visions of the Archigram group's utopian fantasies, with their interlinking cell-like houses, in a series of modular ceramic accessories, made by Franco Pozzi de Gallarate and designed by Ambrogio Pozzi.

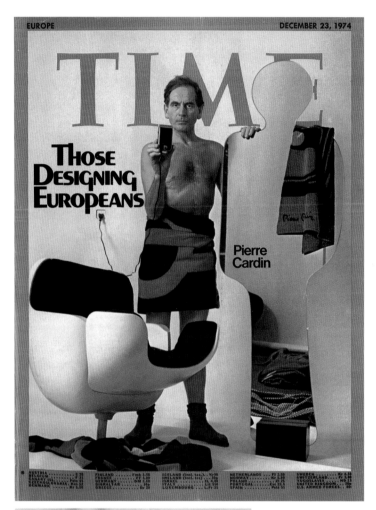

ABOVE, FROM TOP TO BOTTOM Pierre Cardin and his Environment design, cover of *Time* magazine of 23 December 1974; On the Trocadéro parvis in Paris, a bicycle designed by Pierre Cardin's Design Studio and produced for Japan, circa 1970.

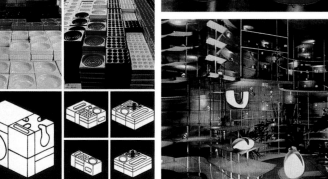

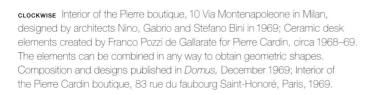

CLOCKWISE Interior of the Pierre boutique, 10 Via Montenapoleone in Milan, designed by architects Nino, Gabrio and Stefano Bini in 1969; Ceramic desk elements created by Franco Pozzi de Gallarate for Pierre Cardin, circa 1968–69. The elements can be combined in any way to obtain geometric shapes. Composition and designs published in *Domus,* December 1969; Interior of the Pierre Cardin boutique, 83 rue du faubourg Saint-Honoré, Paris, 1969.

Simultaneously, Cardin's design revolution turned to architecture. For the Paris showcase of his 1968 prêt-à-porter collection, already shown in the United States and Japan, Pierre Cardin contacted the Bini brothers, architects whose real-life literary personae betrayed the depths of their imaginations. Nino, Gabrio and Stefano decorated the interior of 83 rue du faubourg Saint-Honoré, to create a boutique-*cum*-atrium, composed of two hundred lights and a thousand strips of stainless steel shelving, that was unveiled in *Domus* in March 1969. Designed to display articles to their best advantage, the somewhat ostentatious architecture of the boutique had a short sell-by date and the premises were vacated for a children's wear retailer. The architectural adventure did not stop here. In utmost secrecy, Cardin had the most outrageous boutique possible created in Milan by the same architects who once more deployed their never-ending utopian dreams. The result was organic, yet futuristic, hybrid yet galactic, a technological dream-space indescribable to the point that Stanley Kubrick could well have filmed *2001: A Space Odyssey* there.

In 1970, Cardin took his design armada one step further with the creation of his own design studio. He contacted the theoretician, designer and graphic artist Alain Carré, who had created the Waterman logo, and Helium's famous spherical hi-fi units and asked him to create the studio at the recently purchased Théâtre des Ambassadeurs in Avenue Gabriel. Cardin wanted an exhibition area, gallery, restaurant, movie theater and live theater. The studio would become the celebrated Espace Cardin. As one 1970 headline ran: "Pierre Cardin Sharpens his Claws".

The press that year featured photos of his new creations, which had now extended to household items and tables. His design universe had drawn attention in the USA, with an April feature in the American journal *Interiors*. His work enjoyed its first US outing in New York, where models were displayed at 979 Third Avenue. Cardin kept up the pressure on the burgeoning world market and the studio produced a bicycle for the Japanese and a range of graphically dynamic fabrics under the Environment logo that combined pop and Japanese influences, described by *Interior Design* as "punchy but not pushy".

Throughout the year, Pierre Cardin's creations extended further still and he adapted his logo for a series of mass-market plastic lamps, created by Yamada Shomei, and produced his lamp-sculptures, at a time when Verner Panton was designing furniture-sculpture in foam for his own home. Artists' furniture was now becoming fashionable and Arman, César, Adzak and Sanejouand were all produced by François Arnal's A workshop, whose manifesto was signed by art critic Pierre Restany, a man with a direct hand in the Espace's own literature.

With the Espace, Pierre Cardin had established his own creative center in Paris that grew in stature throughout the following year. At this period, the French Center for Industrial Creation was tuned into Eames, Panton and Roger Tallon; meanwhile, Cardin offered Parisians design in its most extravagant forms. Daninos's simple seats were displayed next to Piero Gilardi's unusual "Pierre" stools. The psychedelic imagination of Gaetano Pesce flirted with Joe Colombo's space-time utopias. *Le Figaro* photographed Cardin in a Libro armchair designed by the Gruppo Dam, a deliberate provocation of dominant ideas of taste. The "multi-dimensional" Espace became an unprecedented focus for the avant-garde, and its logo designed by François Cante-Pacos was sculpted into an item of furniture in 1972. Cardin ordered the first "furniture-sculpture" from the artist's collection.

1972 was labeled a year of esthetic revival: a post-war Italian design retrospective, the legendary New Domestic Landscape exhibition, opened at the New York MoMA; the Nagakin Tower, a futuristic symbol of Kisho Kurokawa's utopian vision, was built in Tokyo. In the months following these events, Cardin focused his attention extensively on young designers. Significantly, he appealed to the genius of artist and designer Francesco Bocola to create his own now-legendary office in the Espace. Cardin now focused beyond the world, to history itself. In an interview with the magazine *L'Œil*, December 1971, Pierre Cardin explained: "What myself and a few rare other fashion designers do is define fashions that in fifty or a hundred years time will represent what civilization was in 1970." That year, *Vogue* had presented Cardin's Roulette pants with tiny wheels and imported Nani Prina's innovations from Italy, both tributes to his avant-garde philosophy.

In 1975, Pierre Cardin not only extended his influence to car design, fitting the interior of the Sbarro, he also extended his dominion, creating a new 5,382 sq. ft. space entirely dedicated to his vision of the contemporary design scene. The gallery, located 29 rue du faubourg Saint-Honoré, displayed furniture, sculpture, carpets and paintings, but also luggage and household linen: utility blended with art. January 1975, a *Vogue* article emphasized that the space was used to exhibit "ideas the creator likes (avant-garde as well as classical), objects he has designed himself or had designed by others, those he has chosen or brought home from his travels, and pieces by artists that he seeks to promote [. . .] enabling young creators to support themselves". Among the array of mass-produced goods, one-offs by Bocola, Serge Manzon, Jacques Grange and Alain Carré shared pride of place.

In terms of design perspectives, this new approach struck a chord. Pierre Cardin's insouciant futuristic furniture flouted the insipid conventions of the time. Even when bodies were swathed in rich,

ABOVE, FROM TOP TO BOTTOM Maryse Gaspard, Pierre Cardin's star model, posing on Paris's Trocadéro parvis in front of a polyester resin weathervane sculpture by François Cante-Pacos, circa 1970–71; Model posing before the Espace Pierre Cardin logo, designed by François Cante-Pacos, 1971.

CLOCKWISE Pierre Cardin standing in front of the logo of the Espace Pierre Cardin that would become one of his brand's major emblems, circa 1971; Male models posing in front of the Kosice Hydrospatial City, 1971; Dario Villalba installing one of his sculptures for his personal exhibition at the Espace Pierre Cardin. The exhibition was organized in collaboration with the art critic Pierre Restany, 1973; Presentation of Italian design at the Espace Pierre Cardin. Gaetano Pesce's red armchair is visible in the background. In the middle ground, a lamp sculpture by artist and designer Francesco Bocola, which starred in the movie *Di Fanta Scenza* in 1972. In the foreground, a roll chair by Joe Colombo, and the Weber and Pullirsch workshop Boa, wrapped round an island of plants; Models wearing striped jersey Cosmocorps outfits with wool strap skirts, winter collection 1968; View of the Dario Villalba exhibition, 1973.

CLOCKWISE Pierre Cardin's office in the basement of the Espace. Furniture by Francesco Bocola, including an electronic desk, an Œil television, a seat, shelving unit and lamp, one-offs by Pierre Cardin, circa 1971–73. In the foreground, a Nina Prani seat; Cinema seats designed by Francesco Bocola for the Espace projection room, 1972–73; Pierre Cardin on stage at the Espace Theater, standing in front of the décor for Jean Genet's play *Les Bonnes*, March 1971; View of the Espace Pierre Cardin restaurant, circa 1971.

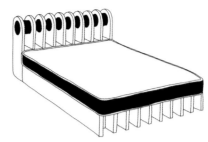

CLOCKWISE Handbag, 1969; Line drawing of a Cardin bed created in Japan. The head of the bed is composed of slats marked with colored stickers, created by Pierre Cardin's own design studio. Similar graphics featured in the design of the Sbarro cockpit and dashboard, alongside handbag zips, created in 1975; Maryse Gaspard and Pierre Cardin present the Sbarro automobile at the 62nd French National Motor Show, Paris, 3 October 1975; The Environment boutique's metal spiral staircase and metallic spotted carpet, 29 rue du faubourg Saint-Honoré, 1975.

silky fabrics, the articles never strayed from their "utilitarian" function. It was a response to Mies Van der Rohe's "Less is More" style reinvented by puritan designers, and to so-called "Styling", considered a baroque misadventure. The debate raged and searching questions were asked of Cardin's intentions: surely his work was emblematic of a hardening of attitudes, Expressionist "nudas veritas" and Miesian "less is more" solidified into symbolism gone wild? Stuart Roy writing in *L'Œil* (September 1975), refuted this: Cardin's mix of genres at his Espace was "like a transparent colored mobile, ambiguous and without boundaries, precise in its forms and uncertain in its definition".

In 1977, the designer's career took a new turn. Cardin already ruled the world of haute couture and utilitarian design; he was the creator of prêt-à-porter collections, coffee machines, hairdressers' chairs and soon lavatories (like the one designed by Gio Ponti). The stylist then synthesized himself, launching into haute couture furniture, unveiled at an audacious new show. The inauguration of his Evolution gallery followed in October 1977, at 118 rue du faubourg Saint-Honoré. Having won first prize at the American Furniture Awards in New York (*Le Figaro*, June 1977), Pierre Cardin used his new gallery to unveil furniture designed not only by himself but also by Serge Manzon, Claude Prevost, François Pacos, Christian Adam, Maria Pergay, Francesco Bocola, Paolo Leoni, Giacomo Passera, Yonel Lebovici and Boris Tabacoff. The Evolution exhibition space was a cross between art gallery and design workshop and displayed unique models with a limited production of eight to ten copies.

Crucially, Cardin's work not only revolutionized attitudes, but also transmogrified the very lifestyles of his wealthy clientele, including stars of showbiz, rich businessmen, elegant society women, and esthetes such as the interior designers Charles Ratton and Henri Samuel. Among his clients was also the auctioneer Maurice Rheims, a man with an exceptional gift for discovering new talent and resurrecting forgotten styles; in a 1979 article, he praised Cardin's furniture to the heavens, comparing it for quality to the work of Crescent and Rupert Carabin.

1978: the Cardin world invasion continued: among his forays, a first visit to China, and the design of the West Wind executive jet. In New York, freedom reigned; Rem Koolhaas was taking huge bites out of the Big Apple, and Studio 54 was shaking its booty to a disco beat. Cardin opened his own three-story boutique in the heart of Manhattan, a multi-genre concept store with furniture sprawling majestically among clothing and art works. In the same year, he transformed the furniture world as he had transformed that of fashion and coined the term *sculpture utilitaire*: "because every shape has a function". It was a time when the French were

spending a record 25% of their household budget on furniture; Cardin offered them a rubber upholstered desk and armchair.

In 1979, the oil crisis hit home and the collective dream came to an end. Only *Vogue* dared look into the future and asked artists and fashion designers what the year 2000 had in store. As though to reassure householders, Pierre Cardin and Hugues Steiner presented their first collection of "hyper-comfortable" furniture at the Conception 2000 exhibition at the Espace Cardin, which opened 2 October 1979. The furniture had removable zipped covers, like the dresses worn to the Palace nightclub, where tomorrow's fashion worn by the most elegant would shimmy until the small hours.

A year later in 1980, Pierre Cardin's revolution took hold on a national scale. The designer gave everybody a lesson in the perception of furniture when invited by the French Ministry of Industry to regenerate the furniture industry in France's eastern Vosges region. Cardin furniture was featured displayed at the Sicob office and business fair and the annual national furniture exhibition. His latest *sculpture utilitaire,* or "utilitarian sculpture", composed at his own Saint-Ouen workshop to the north of Paris, now included "refrigerated" furniture and mini-bars to satisfy the new whims of the occupants of interiors dominated by TV. It was now virtually possible to create your own fully equipped Cardin brand house from top to bottom, an idea that one Japanese businessman turned into reality. From foundations to interior architecture, floors, ceilings, carpets and storage units, the 100% Cardin home was created, fully satisfying the Cardin obsession of at least one happy consumer.

Throughout the 1980s, Pierre Cardin's wooden furniture celebrated the glory of craftsmanship as well as mass production and never lost its sense of quality. The history of art had sounded

the death knell of plastic and was taking a new look at Art Deco. Wood was everywhere, taking on modern virtues. Postmodernists set out to discredit furniture that was "too plastic" and emblematic of 1960s and early 1970s mass production. A dazzling maze of wooden furniture was created under a banner reading: "Anything is Possible". Plastic did not cede ground totally to wood as lamination was used to show off the wonders of plywood and its new, deliberately plain patterns. In this revivalist climate, Pierre Cardin released a previously unseen prototype, a cheval glass, with a fragile metal structure embracing a body of jersey knit wool. Furniture became fabric as Alessandro Mendini painted his chests of drawers in the Kandinsky style and Isabelle Hebey provided the color for a Honda motorbike. Design had come full circle; the experience was complete. Pierre Cardin was now a creator of style, ideas and form, a stylist negotiating the future. The foundations of his dream had revealed a form of design that both attracted and repelled any kind official history with its shaky narrative.

Throughout his career, Pierre Cardin's convictions as an entrepreneur and his imagination as a designer helped him achieve the improbable: to design furniture inspired from his own fashions that only a mischievous eye could penetrate. Alongside André Courrèges and Paco Rabanne, Cardin single-handedly took on the conquest of new bodies and contemporary interiors. While Christian Dior believed that "Living in a house that does not look like you is like wearing someone else's clothes", Pierre Cardin took his own clothes and dressed interiors and minds as well as bodies. The furniture that follows in this work tells the story of a character with a gift for ubiquity. Like freeriding, net art, blogs and crump, Cardin was a vector for new esthetic sensations that this work aims above all to restore to consciousness. ■

pierre cardin

FACING PAGE, FROM TOP TO BOTTOM Pierre Cardin with Salvador Dali (right) and Baron Guy de Rothschild (left), at the Hôtel Lambert, circa 1970; Fantasy costume illustrated by Pierre Cardin for the year 2000 feature in *Vogue*, 1979. ABOVE, FROM TOP TO BOTTOM Model posing on Claude Prevost's Méridienne armchair, designed for Pierre Cardin, circa 1978–79; Pierre Cardin fashion publicity, 1994.

The Pierre Cardin Design Studio

Pierre Cardin opened his own design studio at the end of 1970.
Following the appearance of the first ceramics and stainless
steel desk accessories by Ambrogio Pozzi and Pierre Vandel
respectively, Cardin dreamed of increased design autonomy,
and so included a design studio within the Espace Cardin
on Avenue Gabriel. For the first few years, the studio developed
under the direction of the then designer and graphic artist
Alain Carré, who had just designed a logo for Waterman.
Carré's own studio subsequently went onto create visual identities
for a great many French companies (Jean Patou, Bouygues,
Orangina, etc.). Practically all the couturier's collaborators were
graduates of the French National School of Applied Arts; some
were taught by Jean Prouvé, others studied under Roger Tallon.
Philippe Starck also cut his teeth there. Set the task of defining
the Cardin style, they designed bicycles, strollers, wallpaper,
plates, alarm clocks, ashtrays, pens, watches, jewelry, household
linens, coffee makers, cars, computers, kitchens, and bathrooms.
Their work was graphically dynamic, experimenting with
styles and combining futuristic forms. Though the Japanese
influence was never far off, its themes were re-worked bringing
dynamism to Japanese-style prints from the Second Empire.

The Studio also worked on organic and plant forms. Clouds
became abstract; flowers and buds were stylized according to
the principles of Goethe and Christopher Dresser. His graphics
team built the foundations for a "Sixty-Seventy" botanical collection,
with echoes of Owen Jones' 19th-century work *The Grammar
of Ornament*. His prints applied to industrial surfaces were the
example of a new environmental esthetic, the meaning of which
he explained in a preface to a *Cahiers I.D.E.E* feature on industrial
shapes. His focus was "research, based on the physiological
functions of objects, which attempted to subjugate fashion
and technique to "mood". We are well aware that such research
is only meaningful if it enables industrial production to better
adapt to the consumer society of which it is part".

In 1977, his industrial approach to prêt-à-porter was
complemented by a range of haute-couture furniture, based on
the esthetic principle of treating furniture like dresses or sculpture.
In his own creations, the couturier wanted to incite the French
public and designers to be more imaginative with the use of
furniture: "It's ridiculous to place a piece of furniture against a wall.
If you sit down in a field, you don't sit against the fence but in
the middle. If I create recto-verso furniture, it is because it should
be viewed from all sides: back as well as front."

The approach is reminiscent of Kepler who, in his novel
Somnium, sent his hero to the Moon to look at the Earth from
a new perspective to better help his contemporaries accept

ABOVE, FROM TOP TO BOTTOM Façade of the Théâtre des Ambassadeurs, circa 1969–70; Electronic, lighted desk including telephone, designed by Francesco Bocola for Pierre Cardin. In the background, colored spheres created by artist Piotr Kowalski and Nani Prina armchairs, circa 1975.

Copernicus's theories. Similarly, Pierre Cardin aimed to demonstrate the multiple possibilities of the creative process; convictions had to be less strict; tunnel vision had to be broken down.

The furniture Pierre Cardin referred to as "utilitarian sculpture" tantalized the press's imagination from 1977 and 1980, turning magazines such as *Vogue*, *L'Officiel de la Mode*, *Casa Vogue*, *Domus*, *Interior Design*, *Interiors*, *Architectural Digest*, *L'Œil* and many others, into Cardin disciples. The studio produced chests on bases, sideboards that lit up, tables that turned into hi-fi units and chairs that hid their four legs; all swathed in rubber, or clad in metal, Plexiglas, tortoiseshell or silken jersey. Where bare tubing was visible, wood was covered in lacquer. Only eight to ten copies of each piece were made and style took on design, vice took on virtue; the esthetics of synthesis and "constant research" predominated. Materials and techniques were combined, producing chimera with bodies of white sycamore, Wenge, Chilean Tineo, olive wood, Macassar ebony, oak, and lemon wood. In the same way as he invented seamless invertebrate dresses and buttonless jackets, transforming women into birds, chalices, bubbles or butterflies, he also altered the scale of furniture, turning structures on their heads, upsetting balance and taming colors. The innovative use of honey-colored lacquer and sanguine, blue and pale quartz tones and the effects these gave, required delicate manual techniques. Polyester or cellulose lacquers, used by NASA for their resistance, were applied and sanded, in a series of stages, before the piece emerged in its final form. In such "utilitarian sculptures", spheres and pyramids had an obsessive grace. Forms and lines took on allegorical names, multiplying their rich terminology to infinity: the Padoque range, Insecte, New York, Vague shelving, Pyramide desks, Éclair, Éventail, T, Coquelicot wardrobes, X beds, Cube sideboard, Cornes, Demi-lune units, Lèvre, Mouchoir, Champignon, Serrure, Arbre de Vie, Manta, Nicola, "Mask de Guerre", Paysage, Diamant, Nuage screens, Araignée shelving, Triangle lamps, Ballon, and Équerre; Pierre Cardin's bestiary was made up of over 200 models. Amid this abundance, a Junior range destined for mass production was released in 1979, a year before the creation of a manufacturing workshop in Saint-Ouen. The dream of an innovative, sovereign world finally became reality when Pierre Cardin designed the ultimate prototype, assuaging the long-held desire of uniting couture with furniture. The pieces were made of jersey with a tubular framework acting as whalebone, and the fabric envelope acting as sheath dress. Beneath the item's outer layer, symbol and science mingled hypnotically, the very emblem of avant-garde fashion, signed by his own hand. ∎

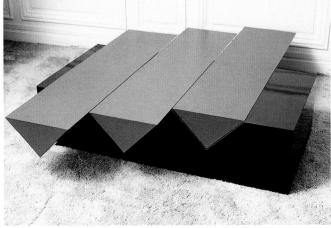

ABOVE 118 rue faubourg Saint-Honoré, Pierre Cardin, seated in front of his rubber desk, displaying a Serge Manzon Balance lamp. To the right is a multi-functional Haut Vestiaire table; its lighted red column is covered with rubber and mirrors, circa 1979.

RIGHT 3 Pyramid table, its surface composed of three upturned red pyramids, sits on a base of black laminated wood, circa 1978–79.

ABOVE AND FACING PAGE In the workshop, cabinetmakers at work
on the "Mask de guerre" sculpture-furniture pieces. The wood is hand-cut
and sculpted, then coated in several layers of gray lacquer, circa 1978.

Collaborators

"A world of solar energy, with clothes as decorative ornaments on liberated bodies": such were Pierre Cardin's desires for the year 2000 as revealed to *Vogue* in 1979 for their new millennium design feature. The double page spread featured a masked intergalactic knight wearing a futuristic flying suit reminiscent of *2001: A Space Odyssey* and its costumes. There were also chairs in the shape of corsets rising phantasmagorically from a carbon floor like freshly sprung mushrooms. It was a vision that Pierre Cardin maintained throughout the 1970s, from the moment Francesco Bocola created his office at the Espace Cardin in 1971, to the unveiling of his first range of furniture at the Evolution gallery, 18 October 1977. The next year, Cardin moved onto the next stage of his vision when the first publicity for the gallery was published in *Domus*, an advertisement that made official the artists with whom Cardin had chosen to work: "Pierre Cardin in the company of: Christian Adam, Francesco Bocola, Yonel Lebovici, Paolo Leoni, Serge Manzon, François Cante-Pacos, Giacomo Passera, Maria Pergay, Claude Prevost, Boris Tabacoff."

The journey to the Evolution gallery started then when Francesco Bocola created Cardin's office in 1971. Bocola had initially come from Milan to present Cardin with the prototype for a belt buckle; Cardin took advantage of the occasion to ask him to create an allegory of the future: a desk in the form of an inverted triangle. Bocola added a cubed shelving unit, a lamp, a telephone and Bulle television with a design similar to Joe Colombo's sphere television that featured in his 1969 Visiona 1 living environment.

Bocola's creation was a shrine to what Cardin called the "4th dimension", and pictures of it were published around the globe; today, it is still the archetype of the futurist style. With technology and Plexiglas, Cardin's multicolored office was transformed into a spectral vision, reminiscent of Villard de Honnecourt 13th-century drawings, and Daphne, the figure of whom appears in the symbolic triangular forms. Francesco Bocola also designed spherical desk lamps, exhibited in the Environment gallery in 1975, before they were moved to the Evolution gallery in 1977.

Previously, François Cante-Pacos had experimented with synthetic materials, creating a thermoformed poster for the Europlastique show in June 1970, where he exhibited alongside Arnal and Dubuffet. It was here that he caught Pierre Cardin's eye, and Cardin asked him to design seasonal posters for the Espace. The Espace logo was another fruit of this encounter, as well as an Espace range of furniture. Cante-Pacos' work is a tribute to his acuity with plastics, their smooth surfaces giving him free reign for corporal, earthly or oceanic themes such as commissures, vulvae, slits, gills and crests. His sculptures have the ability to evoke associations of ideas in the same manner as his furniture, where lacquered wood took the form of a hard shell, cephalothorax or abdomen. His chests of drawers, tables, chairs, desks and coffee tables all play on this organic metaphor, like André Groult's famous anthropomorphic chest in *galuchat* from 1925.

Within this organic vision, the Cardin logo and its interlocking sections were turned into an implacable symbol, a carnal plug that would "logo-tomize" the world. This was also the era when the Archigram designers and architects invented the "plug-in city", an imaginary space where homes were connected to form a single body. François Cante-Pacos seemed to draw on this idea to create "plug-in furniture" and another of Cardin's collaborators, Christian Adam, also adopted an interlinking plug system in 1970–71. In 1976–77, Adam designed a range of furniture (considered "slightly crazy") for Pierre Cardin that included a lacquered wood adjustable bookcase consisting of irregular, hollow polyhedrons, and echoed the designer's early research into compartments and adjustable furniture. He fitted together his low armless Chauffeuse chairs using polymerization to create a sofa. Within the same design current that drew its inspiration from spacecraft and plug-in modules, Christian Adam's furniture is particularly evocative of the Garrett Corporation's 1960 designs for NASA combined vessels.

At the 1968 Milan Triennale, Pierre Cardin had already put forward the idea that furniture had to exist with bodies, as trees live with the wind. The theory subsequently turned into reality and Cardin actively changed the artistic visions of his collaborators, converting them to experimentation: "There is no law defining a unit of furniture. Absolutely all its possibilities are there to be explored [. . .]. Why should a chest of drawers, desk, screen or chair not be viewed from all angles? Or composed with beautiful materials of elegant proportion, high quality finish or refined color, such as wood, tortoiseshell, leather or steel?" Pierre Cardin fell in love with steel after seeing Maria Pergay's furniture; to him, it was "the metal of satin". He subsequently bought Pergay's entire collection from Jean Dives' gallery, Maison et Jardin, to exhibit at his Evolution gallery. Then in 1977, he offered her the chance to create her own range under her own name. The collection of imaginative, figurative furniture, which had forged the designer's reputation, grew with the addition of an Ammonite table and Turtle sofa, a hybrid treasure trove of thirty-four shells from the Seychelles, lined in brown leather, a kind of human-scale Fabergé egg with adjustable opening speed; Pergay also had plans for a giant sea urchin, but the piece was never made.

FACING PAGE Prototypes of the Espace writing desk and chair designed by François Cante-Pacos for Pierre Cardin, circa 1972–73. The wood was sculpted before coating in black lacquer.

1977 was also the year in which Claude Prevost met Pierre Cardin at the *Color in the City* exhibition held between May and June. It was the year that the Espace exhibited one hundred and fifty polychrome sculptures, celebrating its association with the young sculptors' salon and the Jardin des Arts gallery. Here, Boris Tabacoff exhibited Plexiglas furniture in new shapes, whilst Claude Prevost hung a three-dimensional tapestry entitled Hellebore. The work was considered insufficient according to Cardin's theories, and, fully conscious of Prevost's technical capabilities, Cardin encouraged him to sculpt furniture in wool. The result was exhibited several months later at a private view in the Evolution gallery. The experiment was a great success: Prevost presented armchairs redolent of the hypnotic swaying of seaweed or Loïe Fuller's Fire Dance and its outfits that sculpted light. His Méridienne only half-hinted that it was in fact an armchair, like Raoul Larche's dancing lamp with its bulb concealed beneath a veil. One of Pierre Cardin's theories of fashion stated: "the creation of a silhouette totally dissimilar to the body is a process that helps me invent new lines", a formula that Prevost applied to his Ovni, Souche and Lotus armchairs.

In this climate of esthetic diversity, jewelry emerged as an important link—the catalyst for a whole generation of artists and designers. Boris Tabacoff cut bracelets from Plexiglas, Maria Pergay created silver jewelry and Serge Manzon designed geometric necklaces from chromed metal. Following their experience with jewelry—an essential element for the embellishment of the body to Cardin—these creators embarked on a new adventure with design furniture. Thus Serge Manzon created furniture that revived 1920s styles crossed with futuristic poetics. His eponymous range used eggshell and lacquer, reminiscent of Jean Dunand and Eileen Gray, and his portable television and Art Deco radio betrayed the casual flair with which he played with geometry. The television and radio were commissioned in 1976 and both produced in the research workshops of the Mobilier National, the state furniture design studio and workshops. Cardin exhibited them in the Evolution gallery with twenty-five other pieces, including a dressing table and a xylophone-style conference table with insectoid chairs. Serge Manzon also presented an antique-style day bed and structured throne, dubbed "Caesar", that heralded the 1980s "Anything is Possible" ethic. Like Yonel Lebovici, whose Satellite lamp came from a 1969 design, Serge Manzon sculpted lamps inspired by flying saucers. Both were selected by Cardin to represent the advent of "new furniture". One experimented with spheres, slicing through them to create constructivist lamps, whilst the other produced glowing UFO-style ceiling lights. Pierre Cardin first saw the work of Yonel Lebovici at Jean-Claude Riedel's gallery and acquired his Satellite lamp. Lebovici subsequently produced a series of a hundred for the Evolution gallery. Shortly afterwards, Lebovici also produced versions of a lamp, a luminescent shelving unit with glass petals and a tantalizing red, "open-heart" table.

To Cardin, furniture should be placed centrally in a room and meet the esthetic criteria of sculpture without losing functionality. Giacomo Passera's Pyramide in Tanzanian stained lightwood is the very model of this ideal. The Passera prism emanates poetic energy and is fitted on one side with a mirror, and on the other with drawers. It can be positioned and repositioned, turned away and turned round, without ever losing its meaning. Its "indeterminacy of location", a favorite term to Ron Erron and Bryan Harve in their Archigram manifesto, gives it a powerful aura, and graceful, almost supernatural presence.

Finally, came Paolo Leoni and his table, its surface resting on a pyramid and celestial sphere, creating a powerful allegory of the Icarus myth. As Cardin explained about his collaborations: "I needed a wide field of research to generate a creative potential that was highly eclectic and could produce successive collections that were completely different. It seemed to me that there are very talented young designers in France who need an opportunity to express themselves. I felt this was very necessary." ■

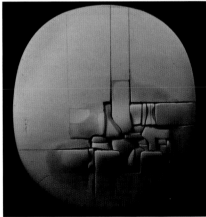

FACING PAGE Pierre Cardin sitting in Maria Pergay's Turtle sofa, in front of the 118 rue du faubourg Saint-Honoré gallery, 1977. **CLOCKWISE** Prototype of an Espace sculpture-cabinet, designed by François Cante-Pacos for Pierre Cardin, circa 1973; Espace coffee table, also known as "Collection", designed by François Cante-Pacos for Pierre Cardin. Bordeaux lacquered wood, glass surface beneath which are placed gold-plated bronze sculpted pebbles, circa 1974; Glulam wood coffee table with relief sculpture, circa 1973; François Cante-Pacos, a sculpture based on the body of a sea creature (1972), a precursor of the artist's furniture.

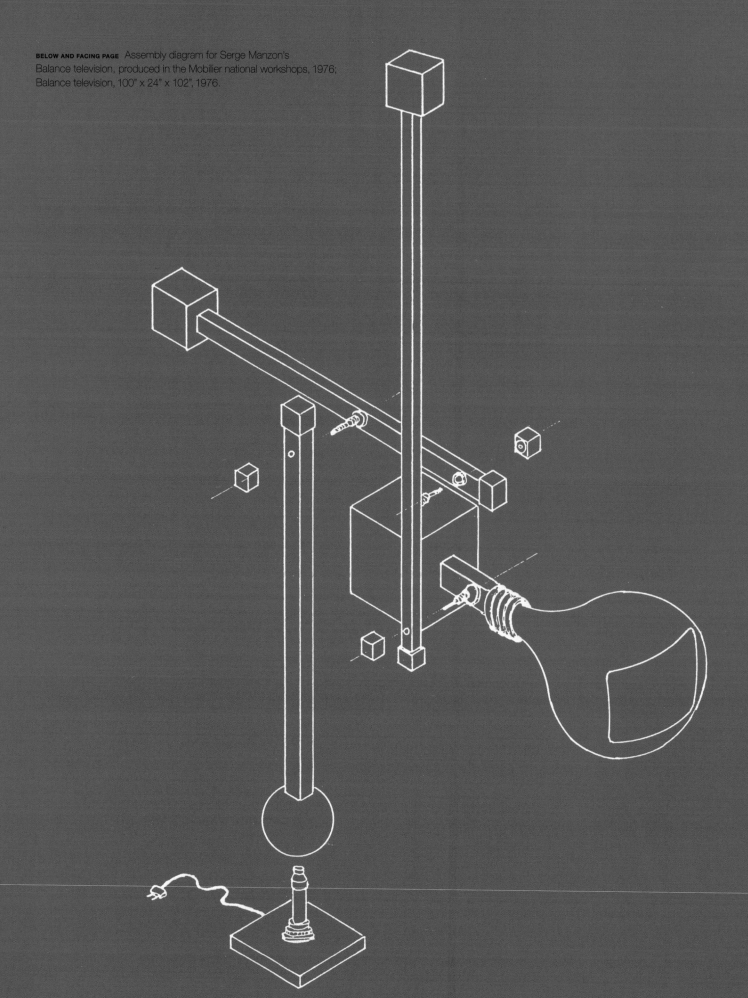

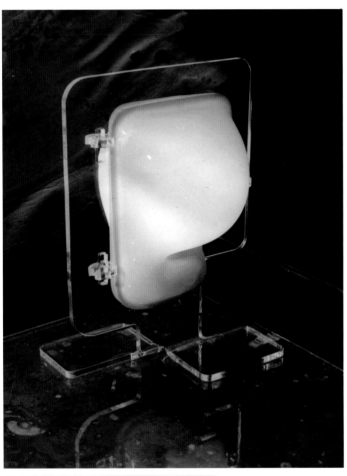

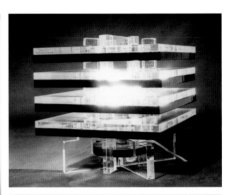

CLOCKWISE Laser-cut Plexiglas lamp-sculpture by Boris Tabacoff, circa 1977; Boris Tabacoff's Arétuse quartz clock with moving kinetic image, circa 1976; Desk lamp in dyed Perspex strips, by Boris Tabacoff, circa 1975; Maria Pergay's Anneaux armchair in stainless steel, produced by Design Steel, 30" x 29" x 25", 1968; Aluminum ceiling light by Yonel Lebovici, 27" diam., 1975; Model for a futurist desk project ordered by Pierre Cardin from Boris Tabacoff, circa 1972.

CLOCKWISE 118 rue du faubourg Saint-Honoré, furniture composed on modular elements, designed by Christian Adam for Pierre Cardin. Console, bar and fold-out telephone fixture in two-tone lacquered wood, circa 1977; Ammonite coffee table by Maria Pergay for Pierre Cardin, composed of a stone incrusted surface, time-rusted metallic mesh in the form of a fishing net, and rock crystals. Maria Pergay range, circa 1976–77.

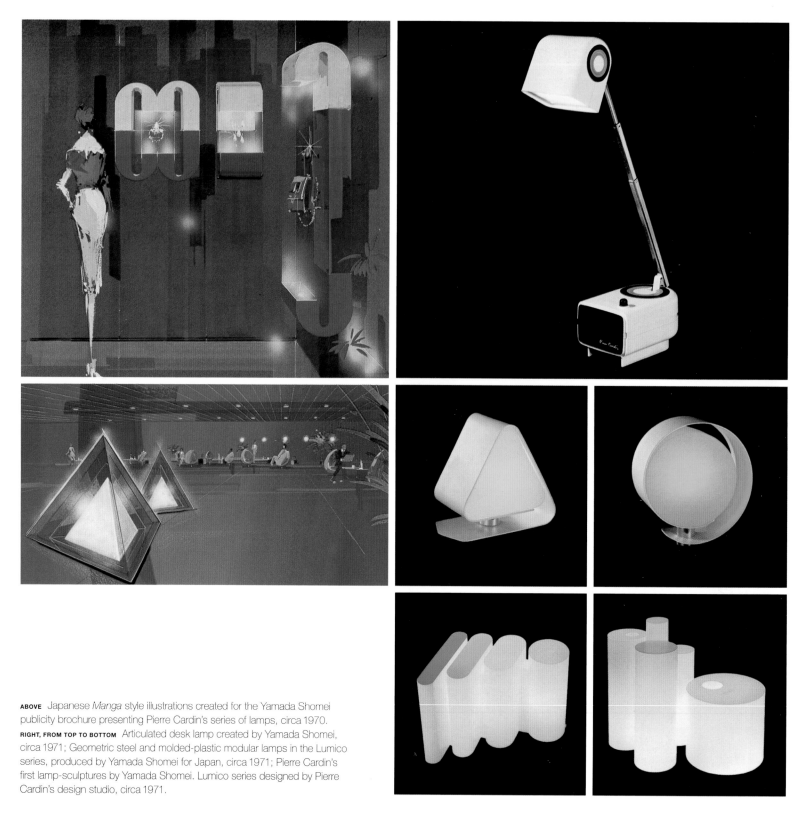

ABOVE Japanese *Manga* style illustrations created for the Yamada Shomei publicity brochure presenting Pierre Cardin's series of lamps, circa 1970.
RIGHT, FROM TOP TO BOTTOM Articulated desk lamp created by Yamada Shomei, circa 1971; Geometric steel and molded-plastic modular lamps in the Lumico series, produced by Yamada Shomei for Japan, circa 1971; Pierre Cardin's first lamp-sculptures by Yamada Shomei. Lumico series designed by Pierre Cardin's design studio, circa 1971.

Editions and licenses

"When something I need doesn't exist, I invent it". Thus Pierre Cardin perpetuated his innovative streak in virtuoso style throughout the 1970s. He was always ahead of his time; he was the first to visit Japan in 1957 and China in 1978; the first to work with prêt-à-porter, the underside of haute couture, that he ennobled defying preconceptions; and the first to develop the principle of licenses, previously considered as cheap knock-offs of a designer's artistic concept. The journal *Newsweek*, in favor of this democratization, endlessly deployed the word "encardinized" to highlight the value of the Pierre Cardin touch when he first logoed his dresses with his hallmark signature in 1969. Cardin's impact is still very fresh in people's memories; his visual identity is still as visible as it is strong. The couturier transposed prêt-à-porter to the fields of design and mass production. In the *Cahiers I.D.E.E.*, he explains his vision of "esthetics and the product in 1970": "It is an aberration to us in 1970 to buy a sink to last 15 years, a carpet for 9 years or a vacation home for 45 years, when such high-tech products like aircrafts go out-of-date in two years. How many men wear the same ties until they wear out? How many dresses reach their limits of longevity outside the museum curator's trunks? The democratization of fashion enabled the prêt-à-porter industry to emerge and rapidly develop. We cannot think of an industry that is not, in the medium to long term, likely to benefit from this same phenomenon." The inventor of Missile sleeves, roulette pants, Satellite dresses, colored flower-embroidered pantyhose, coats foliated with computer strips and kinetic dresses, now intended to extend his avant-garde field of vision to the creation of furniture.

Pierre Cardin entered the design world to diversify his brand, equipped with the keys to fashion and packaging and the word "environment" as his leitmotiv. In the same way he asked Gunther Openheim to produce prêt-à-porter collections for the United States, he also contracted the Franco Pozzi de Gallarate firm to create series of ceramic vases and desk accessories in 1968-1969. Hailed by *Domus* and *Interiors* in America, his incursion lasted the whole decade. In 1971, just when the *Interior Design* review picked up Pierre Cardin's futuristic graphics on his Environment fabric range, produced in the United States by Harris & Co and Kirk-Brummel, back home his French design studio set about developing the Pierre Cardin brand name; attractively stamped Murano vases, lamps, alarm clocks, household linens, bicycles, plates and cutlery. The latter, manufactured by Lafarge and Lapasca respectively, refuted the very notion of the staid dinner service with their avant-garde lines, while lamps by Yamada Shomei established the principle of the Cardin's furniture-sculpture. A series of molded-plastic light fittings, dubbed

"Lumico", heralded an organic, futuristic look, introduced later into wallpaper, household linens by Toison d'Or as well as bath linens by Delorme. Delorme's Equation logo designed by the Studio became known worldwide, applied to TOTO bathrooms and kitchens by Bruynzeel around 1975, becoming a brand unto itself. In 1974–75, Pierre Cardin and his vast product range hit the international headlines: "Lending a name to chocolate has become as worthy and respectable as lending it to perfume".

Thus Pierre Cardin branded everything he touched: from a stroller to hairdressing salon chairs for Takara Beauty, to a bicycle for Fuji. In the domain of vehicle design, he switched from two wheels to the Sbarro car, then to a Cadillac, before naturally tackling aircraft. The Sbarro featured the same esthetic traits as his clothing fashions and furniture designed for the Japanese market. This game of doubling up—applying a style for production in series—also affected luxury vehicles. The "Hautemobile", as the press nicknamed it, was a futuristic, haute couture model, a concept that was assured fame and fashion by the Cardin name. In 1978 he redesigned the Eldorado Cadillac, of which 300 were made. Its thirty coats of lacquer echoed the same principle of lacquering applied to his top-of-the-range furniture. "Only a master can create a masterpiece," exclaimed the American firm's advertisements. At the same time, also in the United States, a Pierre Cardin branded aircraft, the West Wind, was being made. Atlantic Aviation commissioned Cardin to design the jet's interior and the result was a virtual flying-office with black carpet, jersey-upholstered seats, flexible seating, a bar, bathroom and director's chair with integrated telephone. The interior and exterior of the cabin juxtaposed red and charcoal gray. As well as automobile and aircraft interiors, Pierre Cardin created a range of armchairs with Hugues Steiner in 1978–79 with instantly changeable upholstery for "ultra-comfort"; the chairs were said by their adverts to take the user "beyond the mirage of fashion". Obélisque, Pleyel, Vendôme, Trocadéro and Maxim armchairs, as well as Forum and Coupole sofas, could also be undressed, likewise the seats in the Renault 9, another Studio Cardin design. This was fun furniture, furniture that looked like a construction game of cubes, pyramids, oblique or triangular units fitting together with endless compositional possibilities. The Forum sofa was made up of stacked sections, while the Maxim armchair was formed of large pillows placed on a central rotating support. Innovation was essential for interior design to succeed.

Pierre Cardin designed furniture in the image of his fashion clothing, where dresses became hoops around the hips, where pagoda sleeves flowed from the shoulders and where collars

FACING PAGE Pyramide armchair, produced by Steiner, and elliptical Vendôme sofa composed of a pyramid with swans-down-lined gadroons, circa 1979. ABOVE, FROM TOP TO BOTTOM Trocadéro sofa, linear modules that align to the right or left, 26" x 30" x 39", circa 1979; Pleyel rectangular sofa, positionable in a fan formation or as a love seat, 71" x 39" x 28", circa 1979.

were called "funnels". In 1970 *Le Figaro* carried these words, presaging Cardin the sculptor of the future: "I will only put my name to high profile creations that are not already in the domain of commerce or convention. I will place my name only on furniture that [is so innovative that it seems] impossible to live with."

In 1980, the desire to make mass-produced furniture intensified and Wilhelm Knoll created a range of couches and armchairs for the German market. Shortly afterwards in 1982, Gio Ponti, Pierre Cardin, and Idéal Standard launched a range of ergonomic bathrooms. One of its futuristic bidets featured in a *Vogue* advertisement, bears an uncanny resemblance to an intergalactic spaceship. In 1983, Cardin turned to floor coverings, produced exclusively by Gerflor for the Spanish market. As *Paris Match* wrote in 1975: "He is a one-man army, invading us and fixating us, surrounding us with his objects. We cannot escape Pierre Cardin; he is everywhere, in shop windows and in our homes. On all five continents, he cannot be avoided." Thus the licenses accumulated and his interior design work proliferated to the point where his given name became more famous than his family name. During the Pierre Cardin, 50 Years of Fashion retrospective at the Victoria and Albert Museum in London in 1990, the *Daily Telegraph* ran the triumphant headline: "Lucky Pierre". For everyone, the stylist had become part of our daily lives in such a natural way that he was now familiar in every home: the cherished dream of possibly every designer. "Initially, I wanted to create a brand name; now the brand name covers a wide range of articles. I believe my success is total," signed Pierre Cardin. ∎

FROM TOP TO BOTTOM Wallpaper design, Pierre Cardin's Design Studio, 1970–75; Bedroom bathroom unit. The hinges and wallpaper were inspired from the Equation motif, to create a Pierre Cardin "total look". The unit was produced by TOTO, circa 1975.

ABOVE, FROM TOP TO BOTTOM Pierre Cardin with Vivian Greymour in New York in front of his gallery-boutique on 57th Street. Behind him is the Cadillac Eldorado; he designed the body in 1978. Vermillion Cadillac Eldorado by Pierre Cardin, a limited series of 300, 1978. The car's thirty layers of lacquer are reminiscent of the lacquering principle used on his haute-couture furniture.
TOP CENTER AND RIGHT The West Wind executive jet, entirely designed by Pierre Cardin's design studio, 1978. **TOP RIGHT** Dress collection 1969.

Places

Entering Pierre Cardin's universe, we confront fictional worlds like Parnassus and the Labyrinth, so real are they in the poetic mind, one is transported. The mythical equivalents of Pierre Cardin's work are his boutiques, the Espace, the Palais Bulles and his own Résidence, worlds that are in tune with his imagination, where fashion and design intersect. These worlds are like a lost Atlantis of secret hideaways, the initial mould for which was provided by the Palais Bulles.

Built by the architect Antti Lovag, around 1975, in Théoule-sur-Mer on the shores of the Mediterranean, the Palais Bulles was purchased by Pierre Cardin in 1989. Here he housed the most precious items of his 1970s furniture collections, including many one-offs. Its most eye-catching feature is a Roman-style open-air amphitheater near the swimming pool that enabled its owner-patron to stage plays for guests. Symbolism flourishes on the estate: softness and solidity share the same space, the cave is a vector of myth and fantasy, the metaphor of the return to the womb finds its architectural expression. It is as if Antti Lovag set out to fulfill Tristan Tzara's prediction, in the 1933 issue of *Minotaure*: "The architecture of the future will be intra-uterine". Half way between cave and Inuit yurt, the Palais Bulles, as reworked by Pierre Cardin, is an organic vortex, its metabolism engendering a proliferation of organic cells. Its one-square-mile troglodyte metropolis has futuristic openings set within a utopia of gentle shapes providing prenatal comfort; walls, floors and ceilings fuse imperceptibly; its "streamlined" portholes frame the surrounding Mediterranean landscape.

The Palais' interiors are an echo of both Claude Lombardo's chic futuristic decors from the 1970s and Cardin's own boutique, opened 1969, at 10 Via Montenapoleone, Milan. For this location, Pierre Cardin gave total architectural freedom to the Bini brothers, who worked in utmost secrecy. Inside, above the clothing and designer objects, disturbing tentacles of light leapt from the ceiling like untamed carnivorous plants. The boutique's structure was modeled on spaceships: a long tunnel led to a control room. A hybrid Confident chair sat throne-like in the middle, around which elegant ladies would congregate attired in the sorcerer's robes. The boutique, with its white-spattered, distorted walls, was articulated by steel shelving, their shapes reminiscent of mushroom or molecular lamella. Echoes of this morphology appeared the same year in the 83 rue du faubourg Saint-Honoré boutique, also designed by the Bini Brothers.

Shortly afterwards, the Environment gallery, today the epitome of the style of the Seventies and emblematic of the Cardin ethos, opened 29 rue du faubourg Saint-Honoré. "Purple glints flash on and off; discs and triangles reflect the city bustle outside: modern art has descended to street level and touched our daily lives", wrote Stuart Roy in *L'Œil* in 1975. The Cardin Empire's official photographer, Yoshi Takata, immortalized the gallery using a pinhole camera, a stroke of genius that enhanced the enigma of the space. Its artistic directors then added bicephalous images, inviting Rohrschach-esque interpretations. Four steel-edged steps jutted out from the gallery's metal-framed façade onto the sidewalk to discourage window shoppers and those uninitiated into Cardin's world. Inside, the lighting enrobed the objects exhibited and cast haloes around the rose-tinted mirrors, spotlighting the central staircase and its disc-patterned stairs. The boutique window, framed in lacquered wood, displayed works of art mingled with household objects. Genres also blended within and there was everything of which the modern household might dream: linen, rugs, baggage, curtains, furniture and paintings. There was also contemporary silverware, a Gianni Milano tea service and Japanese stoneware, alongside Plexiglas sculptures by Stroll, and paintings by Adam Havas, not forgetting cutting edge inventions such as the flying-saucer hi-fi unit on its Weltrom 2005 stand or Alain Carré's speakers. The result was a boutique-*cum*-utilitarian gallery with 1,000 reflexions, or even a "kaleidoscope", as *Vogue* described it in January 1975, when the magazine revealed how the top floor was actually a fully furnished apartment used regularly for fashion shoots. To prove the point, Bettina Rheims and Alexandre Wakhevitch posed for cameras there, clothed in Cardin.

Cardin had already treated objects as sculpture, and made two forays into architecture, in defiance of prevailing artistic convention. He subsequently repeated both experiences: first in couture, when he invented the three-dimensional cut; then in architecture, when he transformed the Théâtre des Ambassadeurs into the Espace Cardin, a palace of "one thousand and one dimensions". In the makeover of the theater purchased from the Paris City Council in January 1970, its late neo-classical architecture was thoroughly respected, but the theatre was rejuvenated, transformed by the couturier's touch. "I wanted to prove that living in the present was as pleasurable as living in the past", he announced to the press at the time of the public opening. Its solid doors became transparent, its curtains were removed, and the garden was extended into the restaurant, where colorful moving images were projected onto its walls. "I have eliminated everything unnecessary from the space, any decoration that might appear futile or decadent. The simplicity of each room has been restored. The theatre has been renovated,

FACING PAGE Inside the Pierre Cardin boutique, situated 10 via Montenapoleone, Milan, with Cardin clothing tossed casually over Donna and Ribbon armchairs by Gaetano Pesce and Pierre Paulin respectively, 1969.

CLOCKWISE Inside the Environment boutique located 29 rue
du faubourg Saint-Honoré. Furniture and artwork mingle
in a luminescent maze of shelving and mirrors, 1975; The gallery,
118 rue du faubourg Saint-Honoré, its wall covered in small
squares of silvered glass, lending it a nightclub ambiance.
A model poses behind the table, 1977; Nino, Gabrio and
Stefano Bini around Maryse Gaspard sitting on a slatted sofa,
83 rue du faubourg Saint-Honoré, 1969; The Carnivore lighting
in one of the small rooms of the Milan boutique, 10 Via
Montenapoleone, was produced by the Bini brothers, 1969.
FACING PAGE Inside the Environment boutique, as photographed
by Yoshi Takata, 1975.

or more precisely, stripped bare. I also rediscovered sculpture by the architect who built the theatre in 1928," revealed Pierre Cardin in an interview with the *L'Œil* review in December 1971.

The couturier's own office was housed in the Espace basement, furnished with pieces by Francesco Bocola, as revealed by American *Vogue* in January 1972. The inventor's silent temple was adorned with three crystal balls designed by the contemporary artist Piotr Kowalski. The first floor display windows exhibited imaginative forms created by Joe Colombo, Gaetano Pesce, and Daninos, among others. The movie theater inherited some of Francesco Bocola's non-conformist chairs, while the auditorium had removable vinyl seats, convenient for tailoring color to suit specific events.

The Espace staged shows such as *Othello*, *120 days of Sodom*, *The Ride Across Lake Constance*, the Pilobolus Dance Theater, and Marlene Dietrich's last-ever performance (she was a neighbor in nearby Avenue Montaigne). Apart from dance and drama, it also housed Jean-Claude Binoche's huge contemporary art fairs, the first bold events to strike out independently from the former Hotel Drouot. For its opening in November 1971, the Espace presented an exhibition featuring the theatrical and stage work of Fernand Léger, which heralded the start of a long series of modern and contemporary art exhibitions: Krajcberg exhibited in April 1972, Berrocal in 1973, Takis in 1974, Dario Villalba in 1973 and Gyula Kosice in 1975. The Espace also held the first ever, unforgettable art and IT exhibition, showing eighty works from international artists. In a more literary vein, the Sarah Bernhardt retrospective in May 1976 celebrated the latest biography by Philippe Jullian, who had been "preparing his audience for a new kind of art".

Pierre Cardin subsequently reinvented this "new kind of art" in the early 1980s, when he refurbished the interiors of Maxim's museum and restaurant, as well as those of La Résidence hotel in Avenue Marigny. The hotel's top floor still reflects this 1980s feel today and is a far cry from the organic esthetics of the 1970s: the walls are straight, and modern skylights open out onto the roofs of Paris's 8th *arrondissement*. The furniture melts into the multicolored décor of the rooms and suites, and there are occasional fortuitous design combinations such as Yonel Lebovici's Satellite lamp surrounded by Serge Manzon lighting. The first floor also has its moments of magic, such as Claude Prevost's eccentric armchairs by the staircase.

118 rue du faubourg Saint-Honoré had been Cardin's workshop since 1953; in 1977, he gave the space over to design and artists. The "total Pierre Cardin look" was transposed, creating the Evolution gallery that opened 18 October 1977. The gallery took up all four floors of the Napoleon III building, providing a series of artists with the chance to express their imaginations through furniture:

Francesco Bocola, Serge Manzon, Maria Pergay, Christian Adam, Paolo Leoni, Giacomo Passera, Yonel Lebovici and Boris Tabacoff. In this now mythical space, this exceptional furniture enjoyed a setting of perfect opulence: glass floor tiles alternating with dense-pile carpets and walls with small, silvered glass tiles creating a nightclub atmosphere. The Evolution gallery doubled up as both jewel box and podium for resplendent furniture.

In 1980, Pierre Cardin's furniture had its own four-floor exhibition in New York, with a sumptuous write-up in the *Interior Design* review. The following year, an attic story was added; the gallery was a monument in the making. The façade of the Pierre Cardin building on 57th Street resembled a modern Greek temple, a tribute to the careful architecture of Herbert Kashian, Janko Rasic, and André Oliver, Pierre Cardin's first work partner, whose taste for decoration was revealed by *Architectural Digest*. "Simple" was Cardin's instruction to architects before work commenced, a word that became an ethic just as much as it was an order. Cardin's sports clothing, outsized anoraks and furniture eclipsed the marble floor and glass-tiled walls, which gave fashion and design free reign to express themselves in this city legendary for its vitality. The well-thought-out arrangement of pieces, laid bare Pierre Cardin's Manta piece (its name inspired by the eponymous ray) and Serge Manzon's range of lamps sparked the vision of even the most lifeless into life. Fashion journalists flocked from far and wide, each competing with the other to photograph this Manhattan display of French chic from the wildest angle.

In the early 1980s, the building housed the exhibition: *1950–80: One Hundred Painters of the Parisian School*, presenting works by Georges Mathieu, Serge Poliakoff and Wols, sidestepping the pitfalls of the more rigid Parisian pictorial scene. The exhibition opened with international contemporary art, combining Bacon's Pope with Fontana's Lacerations. These works attracted large crowds who were also introduced to a new style of lacquered furniture from across the Atlantic that enjoyed its first showing in America.

Cardin was a designer ahead of his time. He did't need Jean Prouvé's folded metal or Charlotte Perriand's patinated wood to come back into fashion before finding "the right note" for contemporary interiors, as proved at his *Apogee of Curvilinear Geometry* exhibition at Brussels' Espace Cardin in 1983. The market at the time was set on "clean" beige decors; Cardin, meanwhile, was always where we least expected him to be, celebrating the 1950s. "The past is readily reassuring: we have old furniture; we dress old-fashioned," he stated in 1971. This, however, did not prevent him from selecting neglected periods of the past when so desired in order to revive his futuristic visions. Flying in the face of fashion was yet another of his bold risks. ∎

ABOVE The current decoration on the top floor of Residence Maxim's in Paris, designed by Pierre Cardin. The colored rooms house a collection of furniture and works of art. In the far distance is Victor Vasarely's work as well as a conference table created by Serge Manzon and in the foreground, an Eclair lamp by the same artist.

The Pierre Cardin

Design
Studio

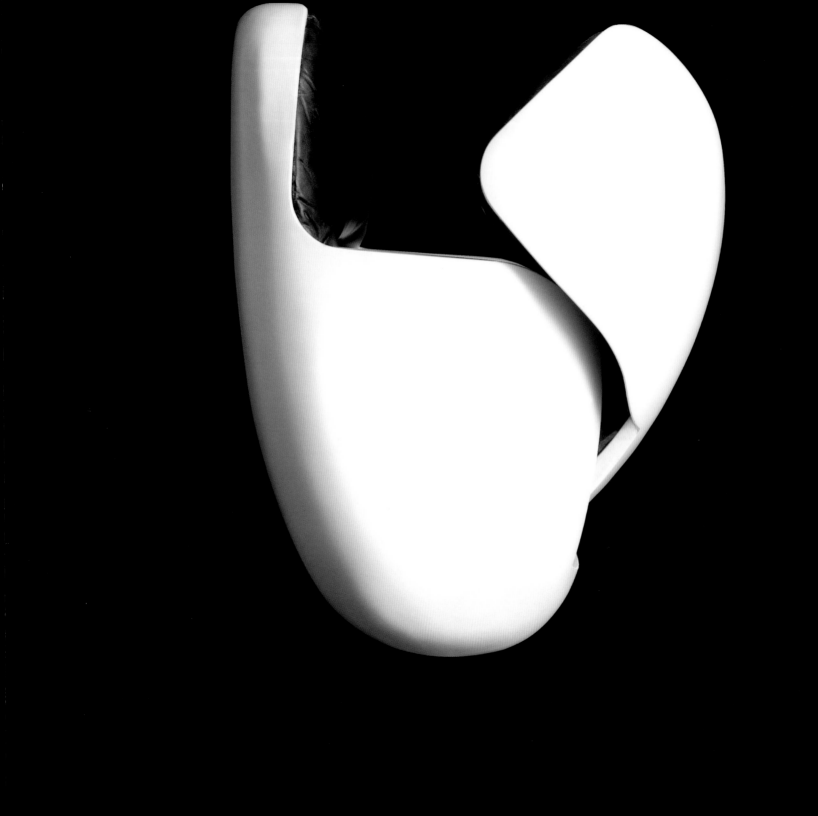

PAGE 53 Pierre Cardin in 118 rue du faubourg Saint-Honoré front room, on the left, the Arbre de Vie cabinet, 1977.
PRECEDING DOUBLE PAGE Prototype for a fold-up armchair for the Espace Pierre Cardin theater. Resin shell and leather cushions, 30" x 24" x 28", circa 1973. ABOVE White lacquered coffee table, 18" x 18" x 12", 1970.

Cube lamp made of seven sheets of Plexiglas connected by metal rods.
The suspended cube is cut in white Perspex, 20" x 15" x 8", circa 1974.

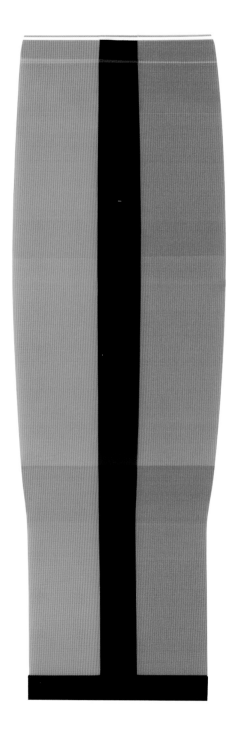

White Perspex Ballon lamp, edged in red with a black thread, 16" x 4" x 13", circa 1978.
FOLLOWING DOUBLE PAGE Blue Plexiglas triangular lamp fitted into six transparent triangles, 26" x 16" x 14", circa 1980.

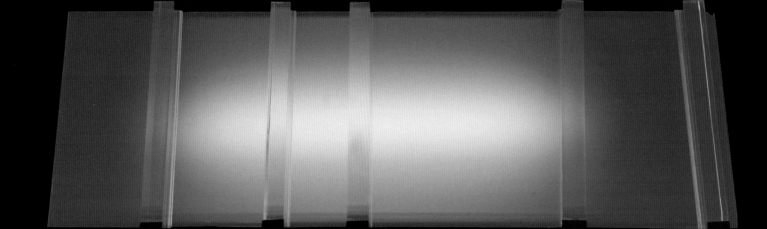

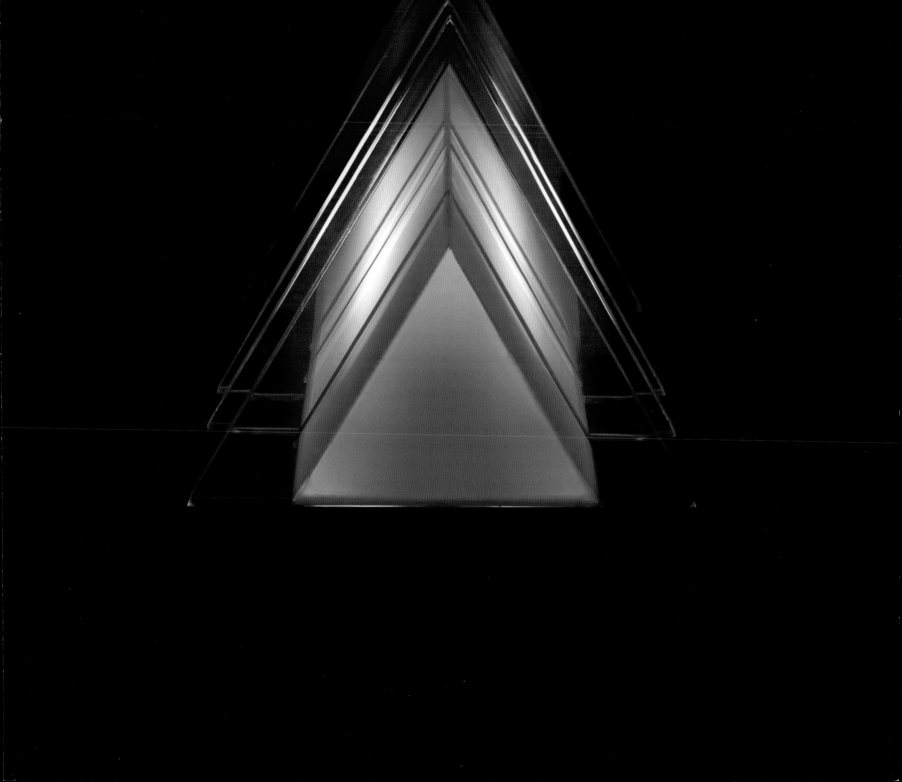

Pyramide television with triangular slots in fuchsia lacquered wood, fitted screen
and control buttons, 18" x 12" x 13", prototype, circa 1977.

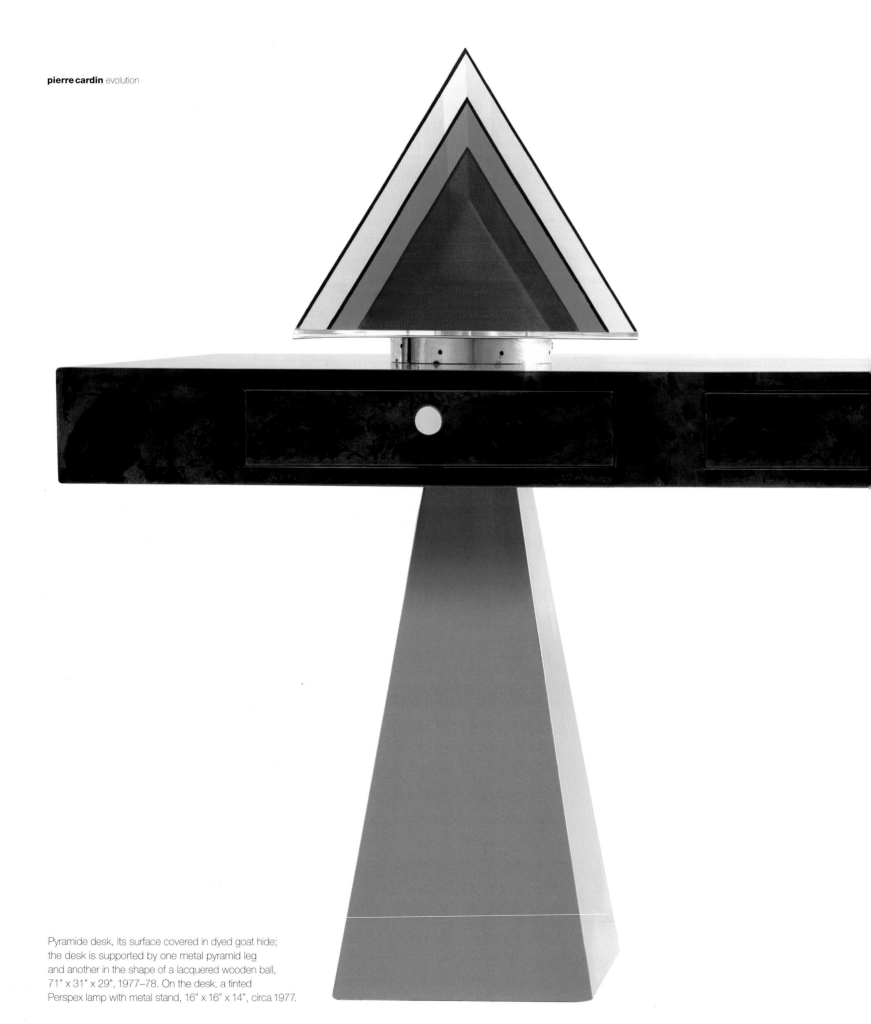

Pyramide desk, its surface covered in dyed goat hide;
the desk is supported by one metal pyramid leg
and another in the shape of a lacquered wooden ball,
71" x 31" x 29", 1977–78. On the desk, a tinted
Perspex lamp with metal stand, 16" x 16" x 14", circa 1977.

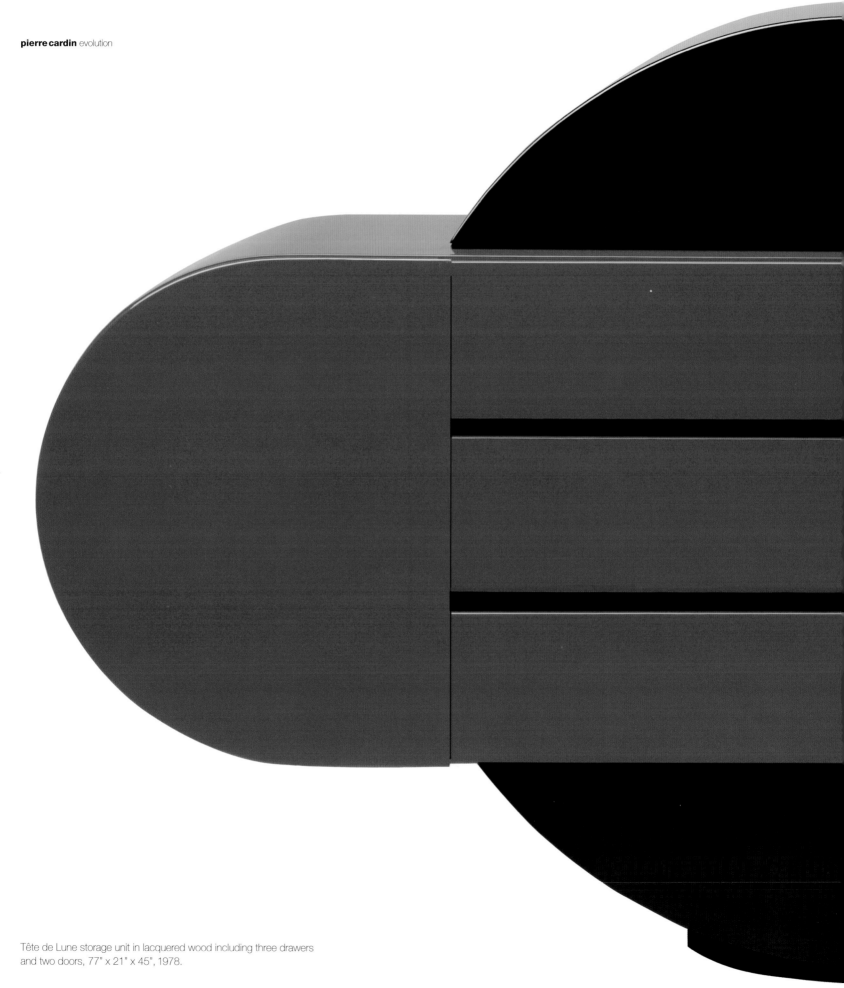

Tête de Lune storage unit in lacquered wood including three drawers
and two doors, 77" x 21" x 45", 1978.

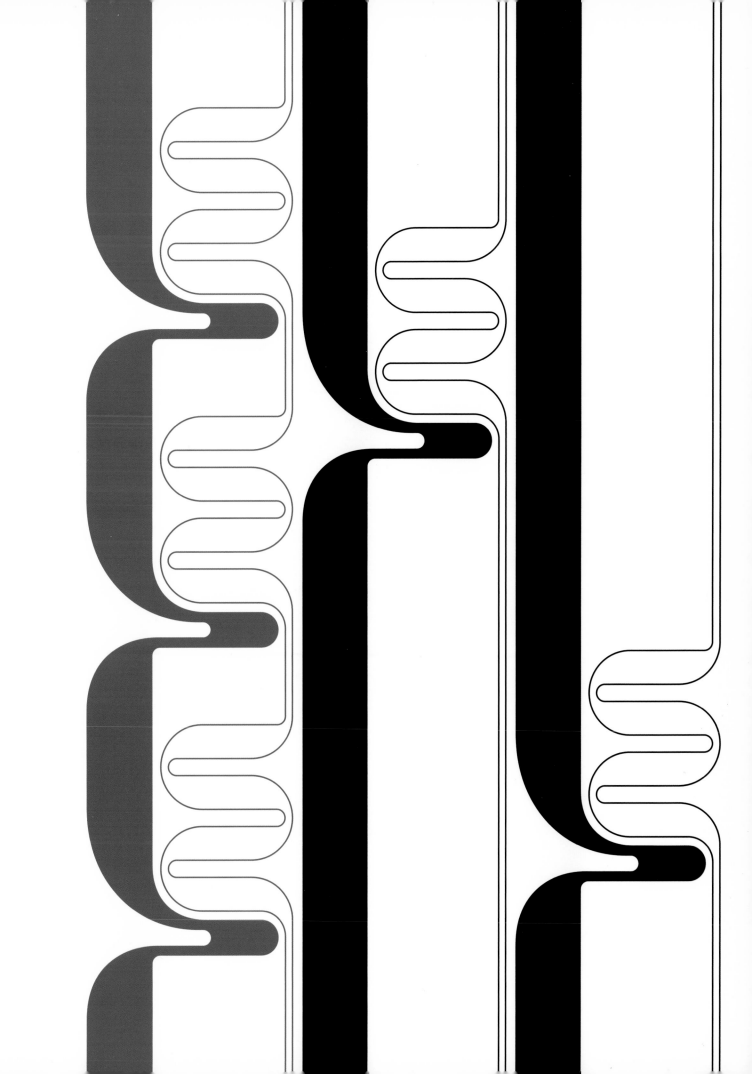

Manta unit in green, bronze and orange lacquered wood, including two doors
and six inside shelves, 55" x 18" x 72", 1977–78. Detail.

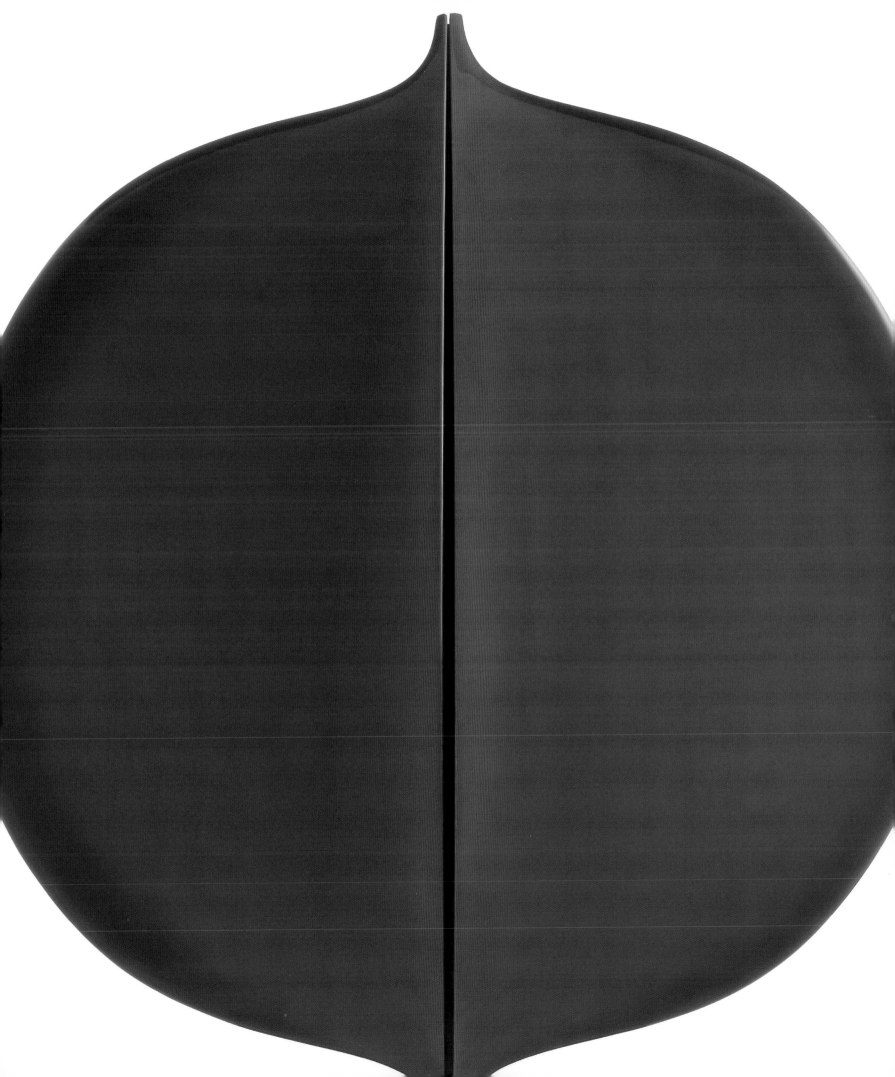

Champignon chest in lacquered wood, with two doors
and three drawers, 59" x 18" x 45", 1979.

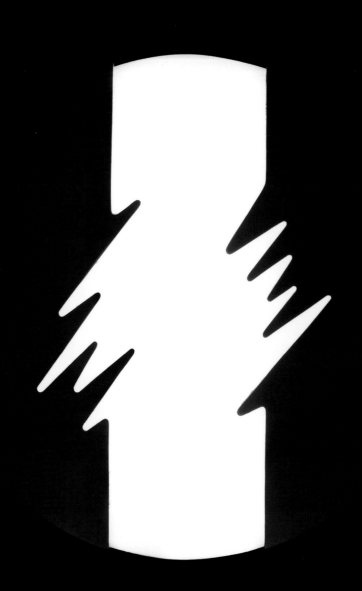

Circular lamp in chrome Perspex with sculpted pattern, mounted on a metal
lamp base formed by a truncated pyramid, 15" x 4" x 16", circa 1978.

ABOVE AND FACING PAGE Triangle lamp with a silver-colored aluminum cut-out shell,
placed on a rectangular metal base. The patterned center lights up, 20" x 4" x 11", circa 1978;
Arbre de Vie unit in lacquered wood on a truncated pyramid base, the central tree design
covers the opening of the two doors, 55" x 20" x 63", 1977.

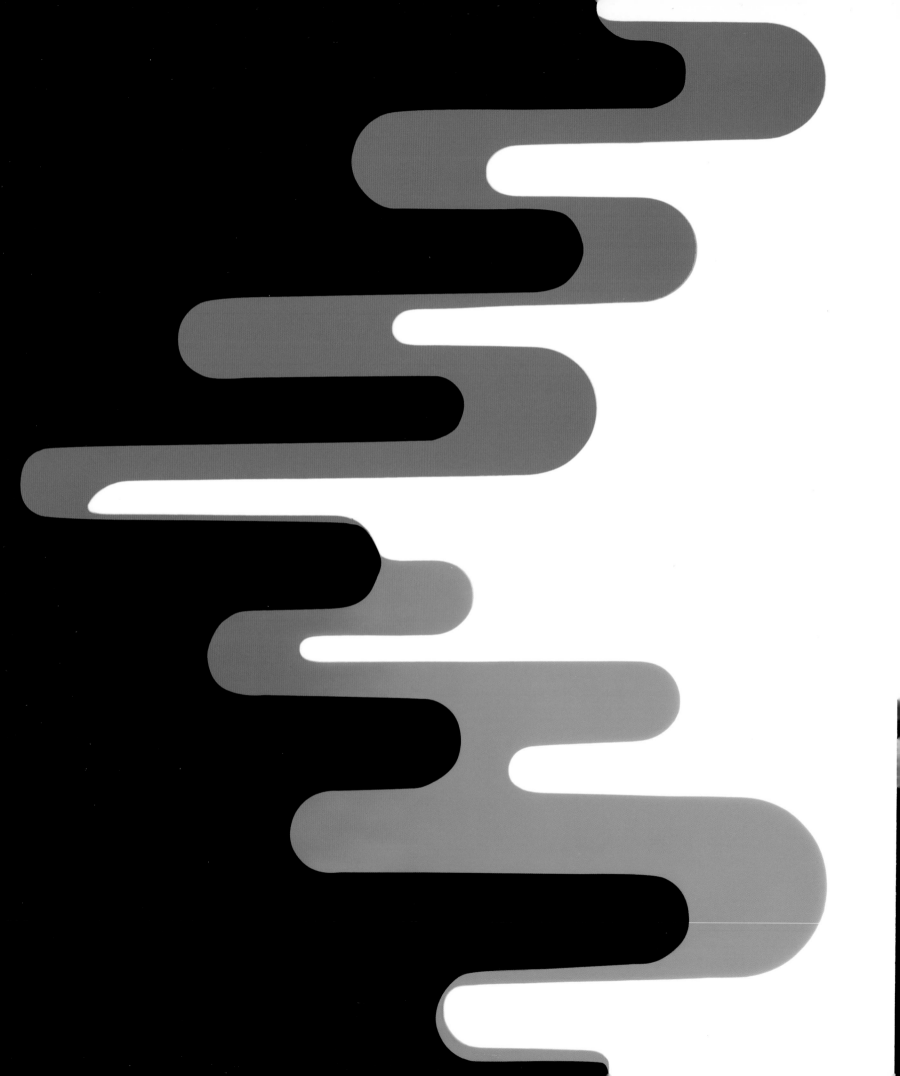

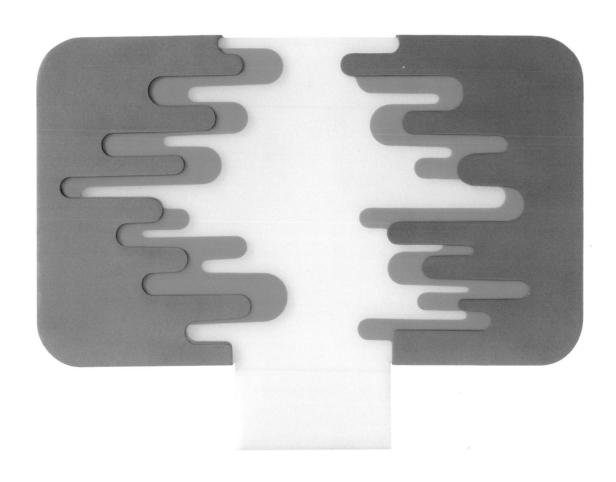

Plexiglas lamp, with a central Arbre de Vie motif, standing on a cube,
18" x 4" x 14", 1977. Detail of the motif.

ABOVE AND FACING PAGE Black lacquered standing storage unit with two doors
and four interior shelves, 63" x 18" x 31", circa 1979; Steel and ebony belt buckles,
8" x 4", and copper and steel, 5" x 3", 1969.

80

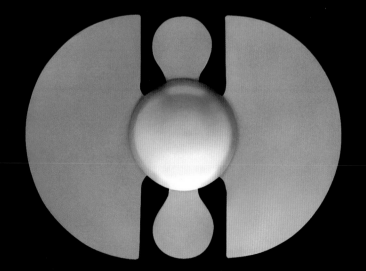

Vague table in black lacquered wood with blue lapis lazuli thread, featuring a sliding top and inside
service unit. Originally a coffee table, the table was subsequently mounted on a base and transformed
as a display counter for the boutique, original dimensions: 54" x 37" x 17", circa 1978.

Lèvres desk in black lacquered wood with two lip-sculpted drawers, 1979 and white Perspex Ballon lamp with a red rim and black thread, 16" x 4" x 14", circa 1979.

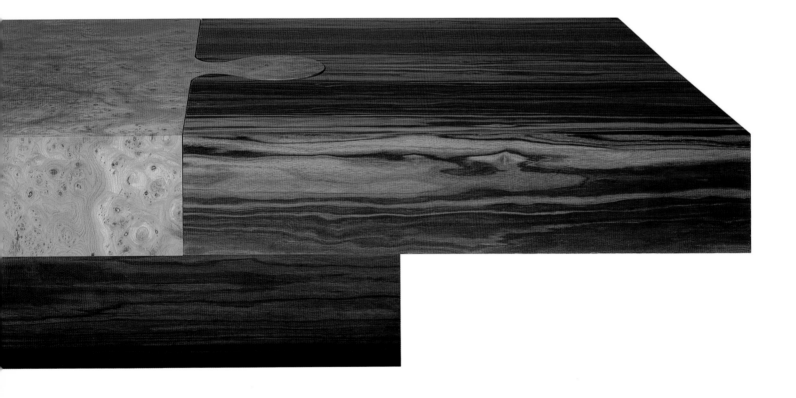

Espace coffee table in lemon wood and veneering composed
of two interlocking surfaces, 51" x 30" x 6", 1978–79. Detail.

Varnished and veneered Demi-Lune chest on a bronze stand, with eight storage
drawers, 63" x 18" x 43", circa 1978. Detail of drawers.

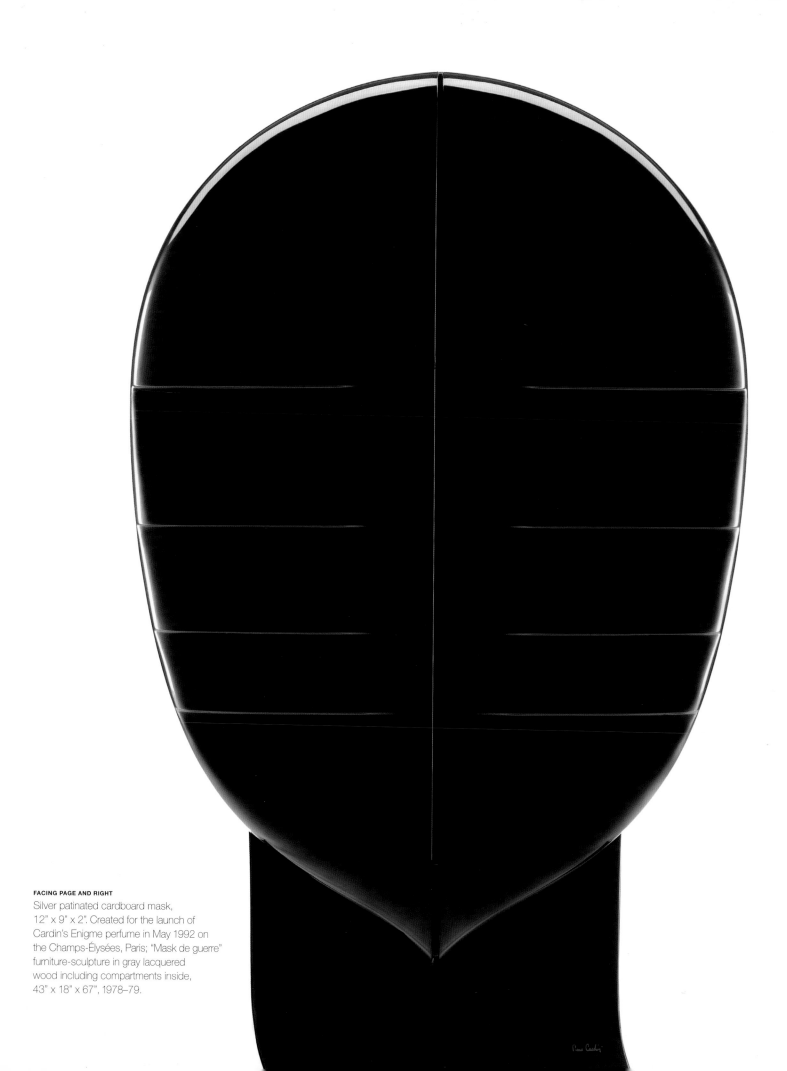

FACING PAGE AND RIGHT
Silver patinated cardboard mask,
12" x 9" x 2". Created for the launch of
Cardin's Enigme perfume in May 1992 on
the Champs-Élysées, Paris; "Mask de guerre"
furniture-sculpture in gray lacquered
wood including compartments inside,
43" x 18" x 67", 1978–79.

Pyramide chest in black lacquered wood with six drawers,
71" x 18" x 35", 1978–79. Detail.

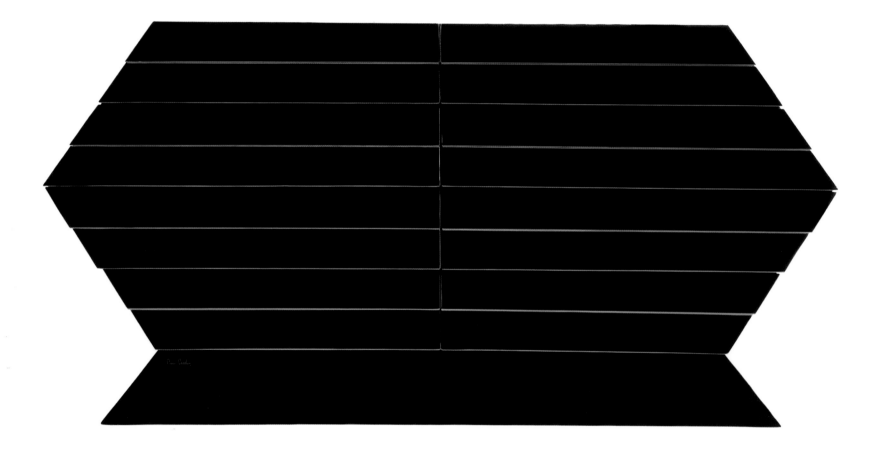

ABOVE AND FACING PAGE Pyramide chest in black lacquered wood with six drawers, 71" x 18" x 35",
1978–79. Detail; Wallpaper design, Pierre Cardin's Design Studio, 1970–75.

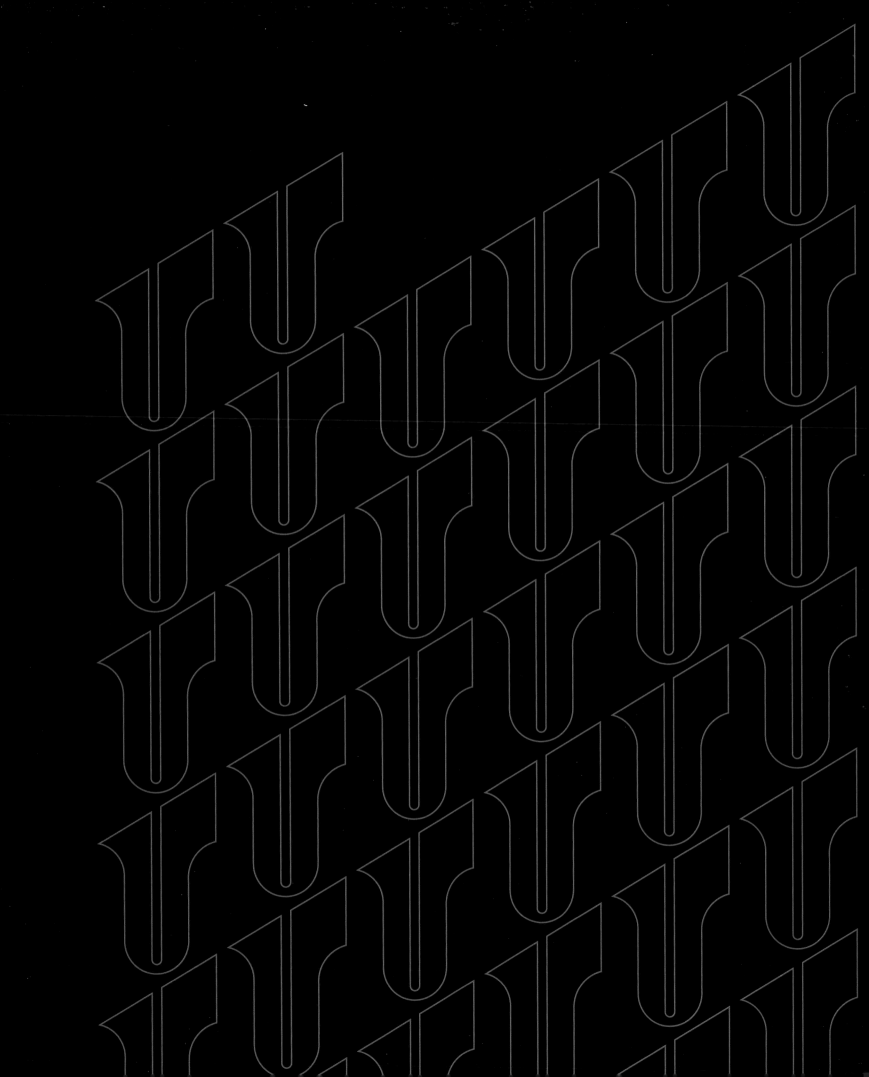

Walnut-shaped Nicola unit in varnished wood, with two doors and three inside
natural wood shelves, 59" x 17" x 59", 1978–79. Detail.

Padoque shelving unit in layered lacquer with four inside shelves, 63" x 18" x 30",
circa 1979. Detail; Large Évolution lamp, blue lacquered wood, with metal cupola and bulb,
mounted on a circular metal base, 28" x 21" x 32", 1978–79.

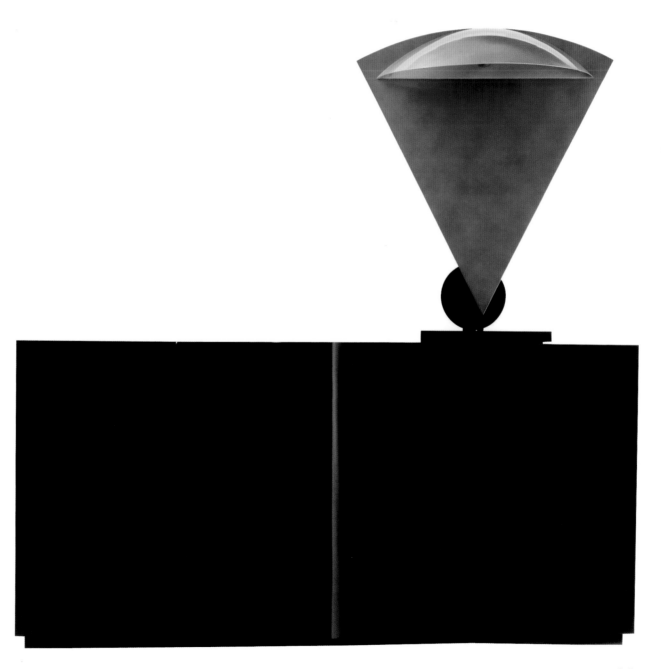

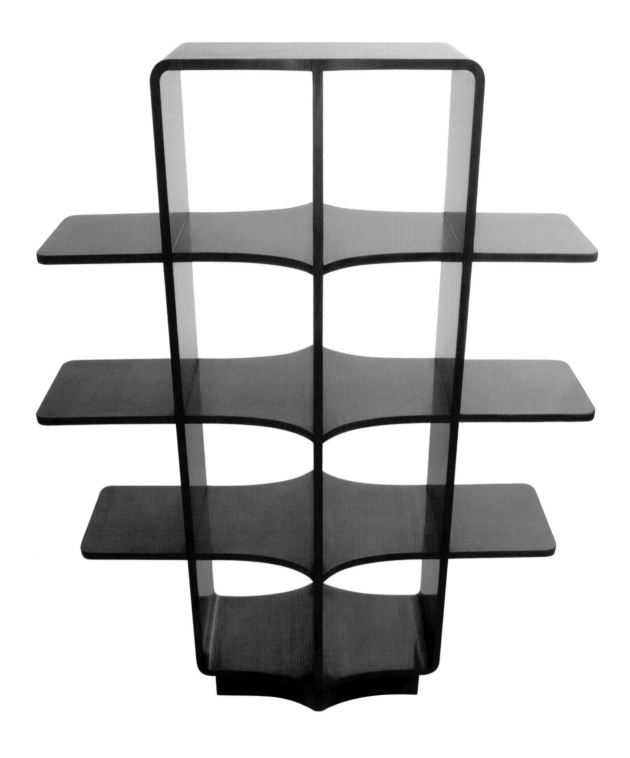

Natural wood shelving unit made up of three overhanging shelves
with rounded corners, 43" x 17" x 59", circa 1979. Detail.

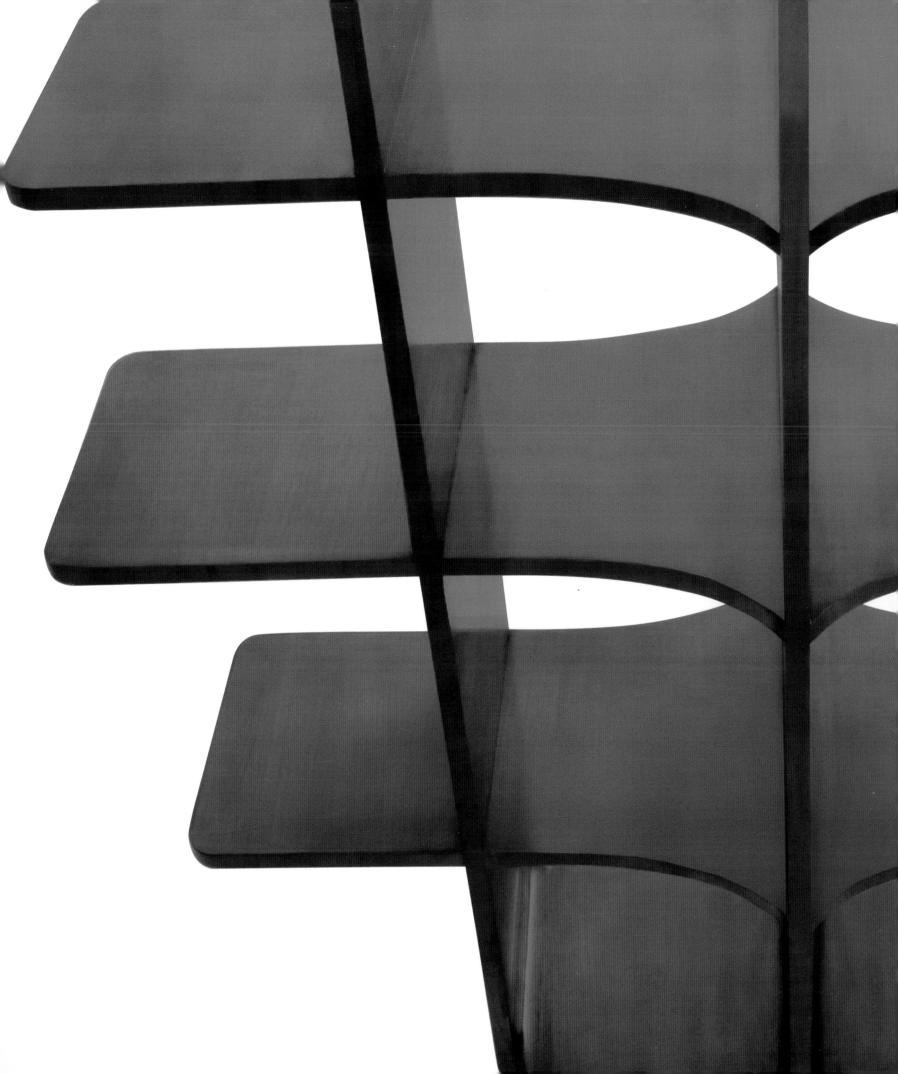

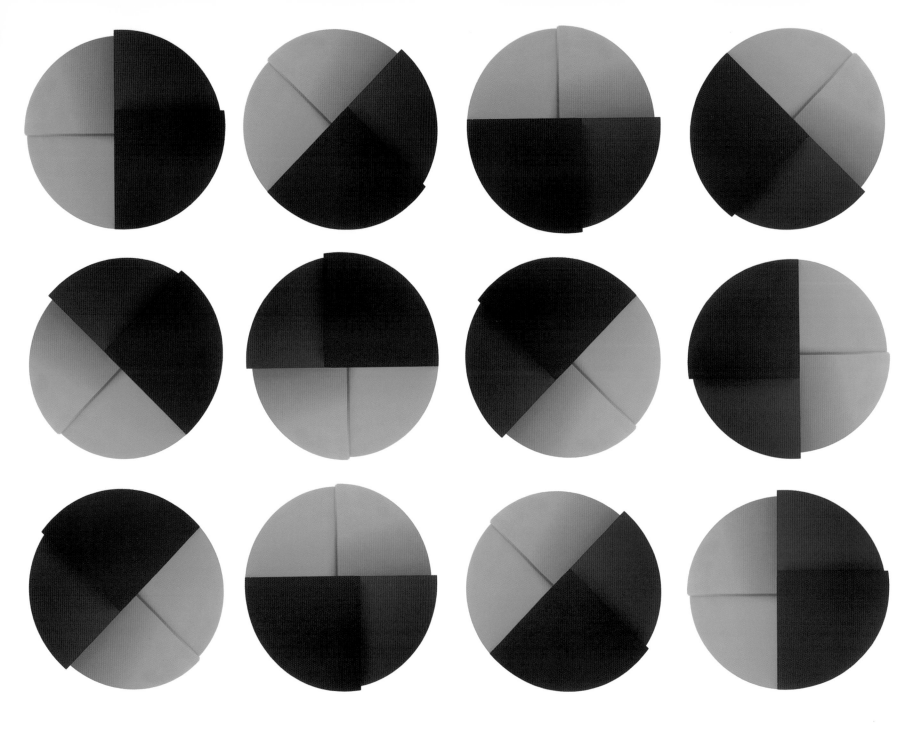

Laminated wood coffee table composed of four trays,
47" x 47" x 16", circa 1978.

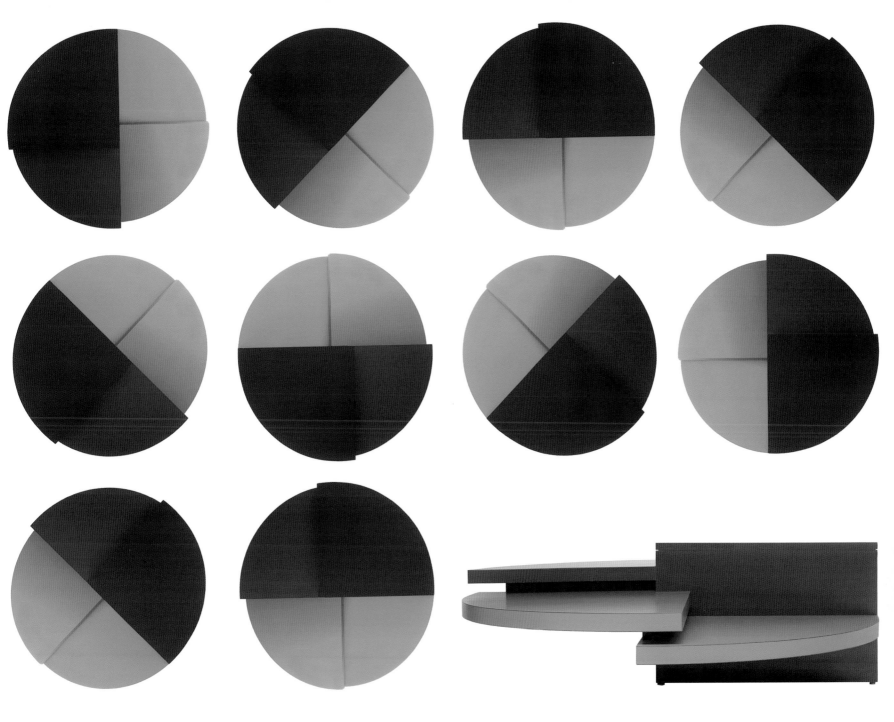

ABOVE AND FACING PAGE Satin bags. Red model 10" x 6" x 1"; violet model 16" x 5" x 0.5"; pink model 9" x 5" x 1", 1982; Straw and silver leather bags. Red model 7" x 8" x 1"; yellow model 8" x 6" x 1", 1984.

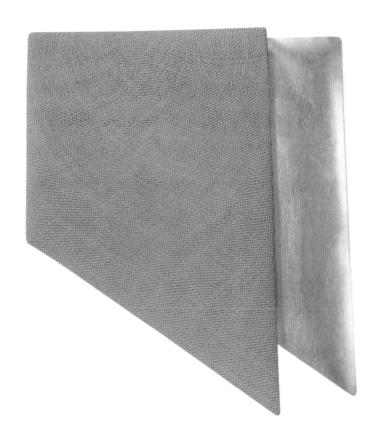

ABOVE AND FACING PAGE Satin bags. Blue model 6" x 8" x 1", 1980; pink model 16" x 5" x 0.5", 1982;
Paysage unit in lacquered wood of three colors, featuring three inside shelves and a circular
figure on the outside. The panel opens onto the pink section, 31" x 18" x 47", circa 1980.
FOLLOWING DOUBLE PAGE, LEFT Wallpaper design, Pierre Cardin's Design Studio, 1970–75.
RIGHT Coquelicot unit in lacquered wood, 30" x 14" x 46", 1979–80.

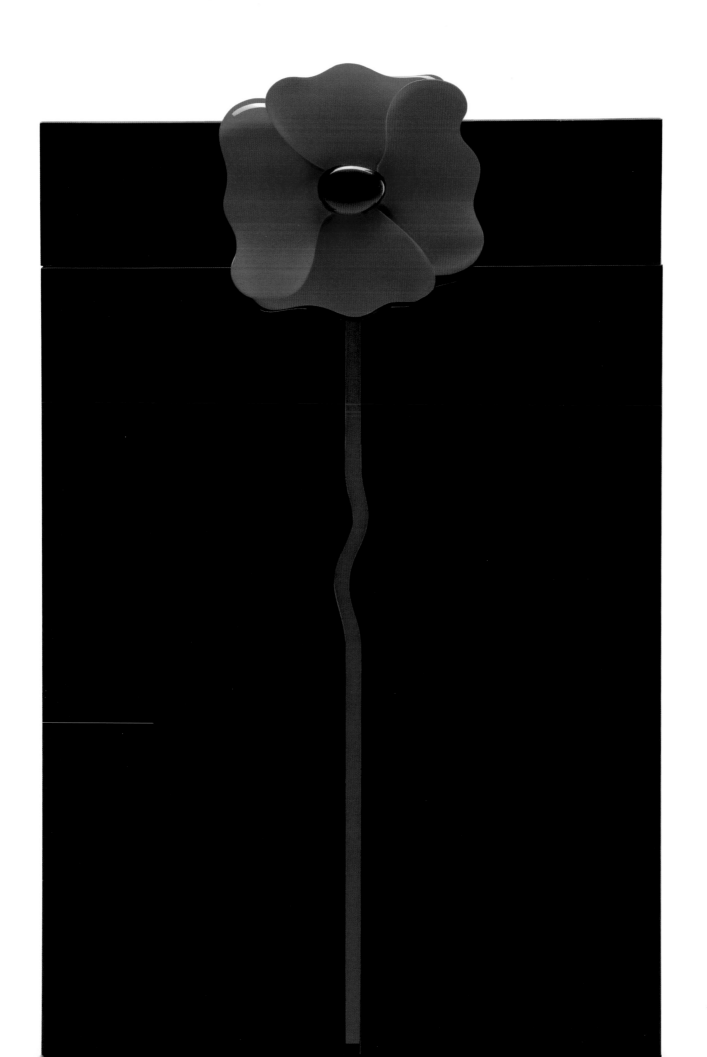

Pyramide desk with a leather desk blotter and lacquered wood surface; the frame and drawers are in lacquered wood; the face of the base is fitted with a plain or smoked glass mirror. 85" x 39" x 29", 1980–81. Detail.

Desk with lacquered casing, wooden surface and base, and lacquered front,
75" x 33" x 33", circa 1980. Detail.

Varnished wooden chair with leather seat, 18" x 18" x 29", circa 1980. Detail.

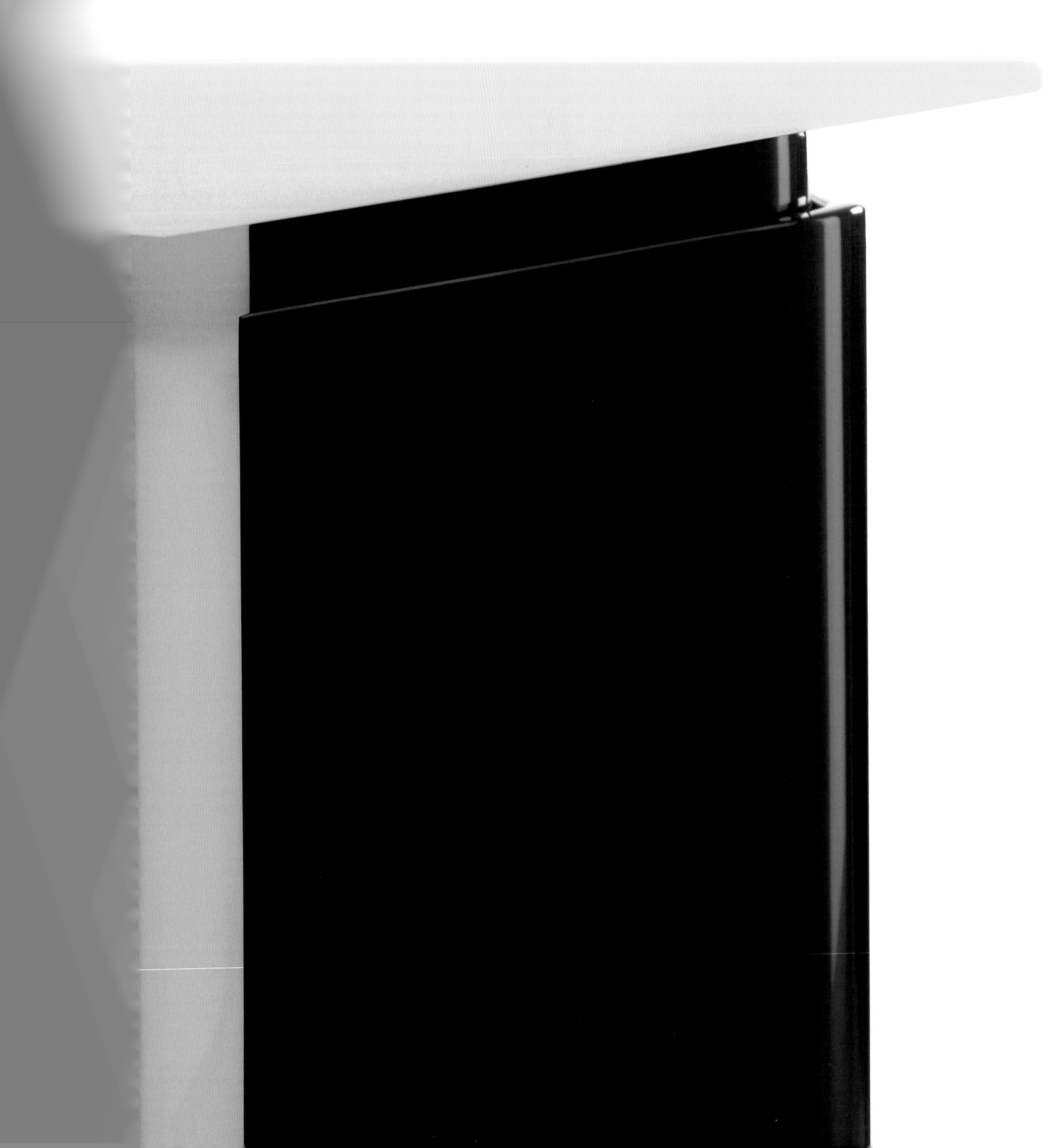

Delta bar unit in lacquered wood, featuring two doors, four shelf-compartments
and fitted refrigerator, 37" x 21" x 39", circa 1983. Detail.

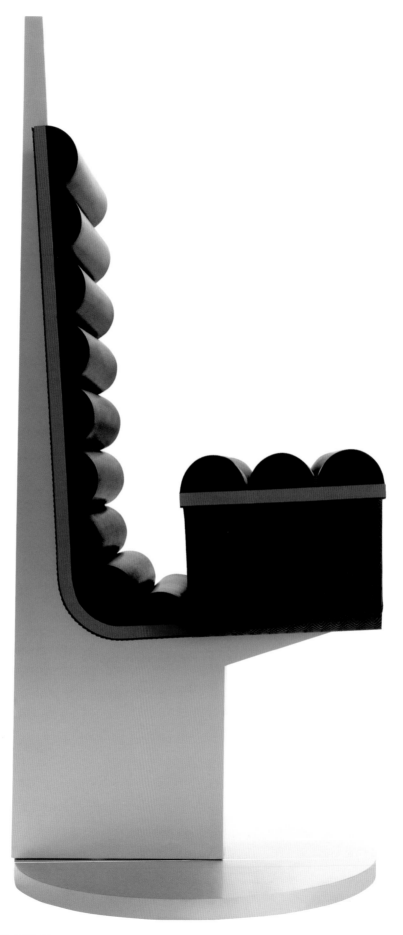

Armchair with rubber seat and back, 31" x 24" x 55", 1979–80.

Junior unit made of chrome-plated metal tubes and four lacquered
natural wood drawers, 54" x 18" x 54", 1979–80.

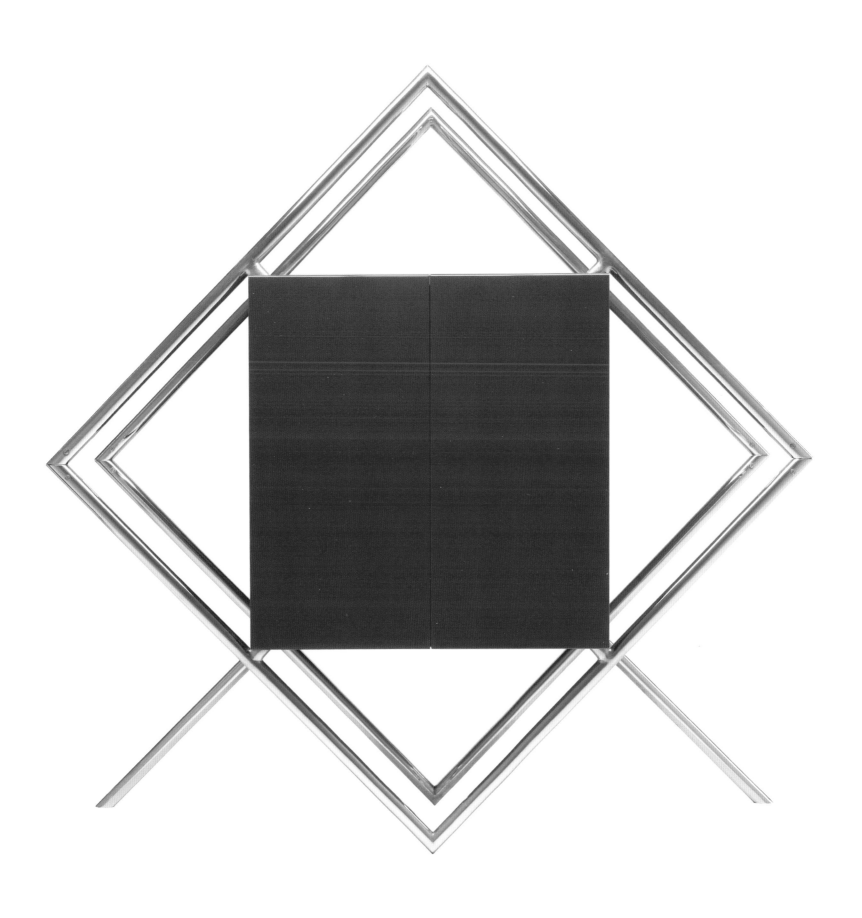

Junior unit made of chrome-plated metal tubes and a cupboard with
two doors in red lacquered wood, 59" x 48 x 59", 1979–80.

Red leather bag with copper and steel fasteners, 18" diam., shoulder strap 20", 1986.

Brown leather bag with copper and steel fasteners, 18" diam., shoulder strap 16", 1986.

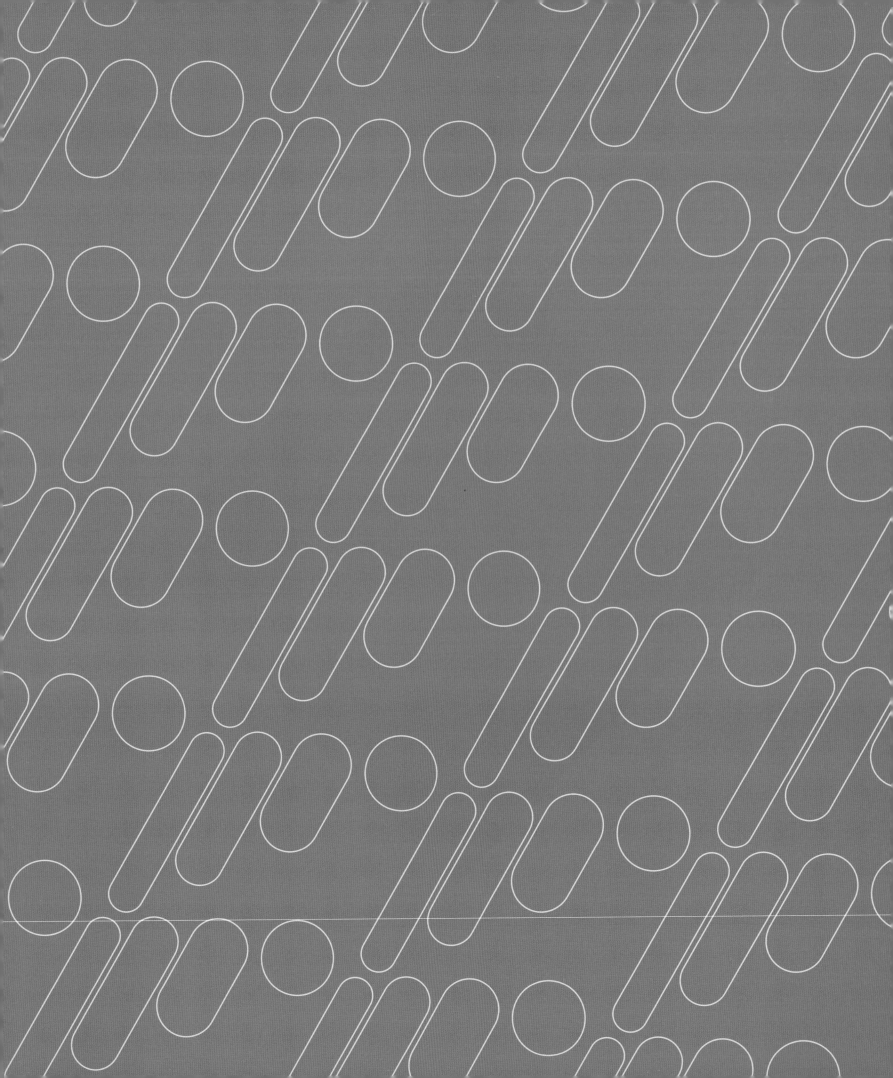

Wallpaper design, Pierre Cardin's Design Studio, 1970–75; T-shaped chest in varnished wood, with one lacquered side, two drawers and two doors, 63" x 18" x 43", 1980.

Wooden console table with sculpted lacquered wood base, 79" x 19" x 32", circa 1980.
On the surface, a Planète lamp by Serge Manzon made up of three sections of gold-plated metal,
and fitted with a bulb, 20" x 14" x 20", circa 1977. Detail of the base.

Black and green felt hats, 1990.

FRANCESCO BOCOLA
FRANÇOIS CANTE-PACOS
YONEL LEBOVICI
SERGE MANZON
MARIA PERGAY
CLAUDE PREVOST
CHRISTIAN ADAM
GIACOMO PASSERA
Collaborators

PRECEDING PAGE Pierre Cardin at his desk in the Espace office.
Desk by Francesco Bocola and lamp by Piotr Kowalski, 1970.
LEFT AND FACING PAGE Television unit and record player by Francesco Bocola
in stained Plexiglas, 39" x 32" x 70", 1971–72. Detail.

ABOVE AND FACING PAGE Television unit and record player by Francesco Bocola in stained Plexiglas, 39" x 32" x 70", 1971–72; Wallpaper design, Pierre Cardin's Design Studio, 1970–75.

Illuminated storage unit by Francesco Bocola in stained
Plexiglas with three drawers, 31" x 24" x 64", 1971–72.
Detail of drawers.

Desk chair on wheels by Francesco Bocola with Plexiglas seat
and chromed tubular structure, 24" x 31" x 43", 1971.

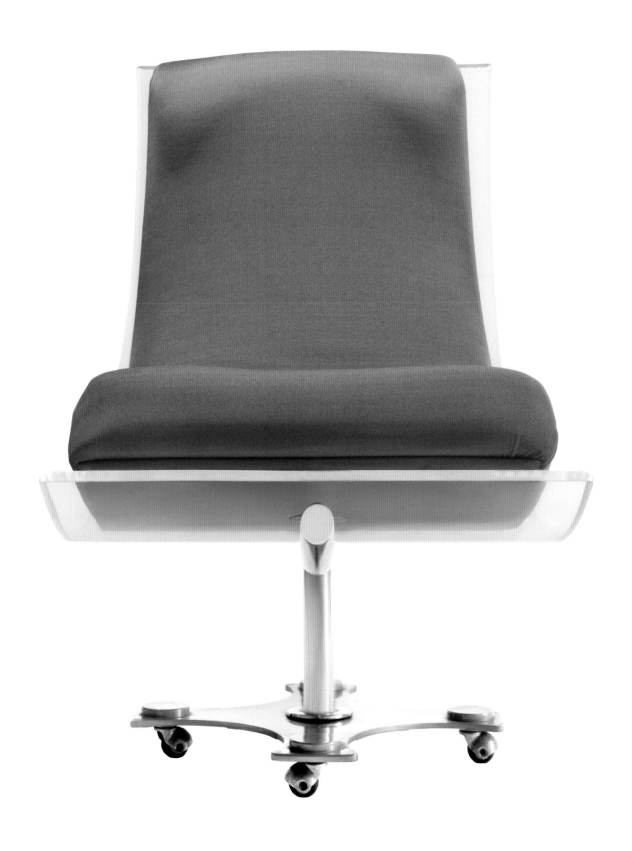

FACING PAGE AND ABOVE Espace chest by François Cante-Pacos in black lacquered wood
with two sculpted doors and drawers inside, 63" x 25" x 47", 1972–73; Espace chair
by François Cante-Pacos in black lacquered wood with sculpted back, 16" x 19" x 35", 1972.

Espace writing desk by François Cante-Pacos in black lacquered wood with two doors, sculpted lid,
and interior drawers and shelves, 26" x 15" x 45", 1972. Close-up of sculpted lid feature.

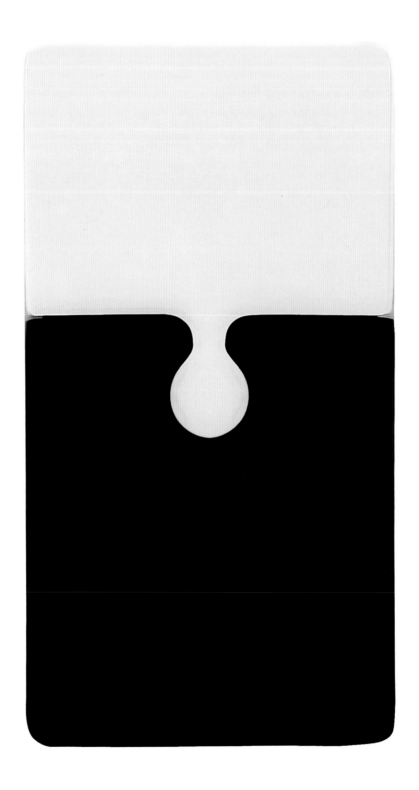

ABOVE AND FACING PAGE Espace box by François Cante-Pacos in varnished earthenware,
8" x 5" x 3", 1969; Detail of a coat in wool with black vinyl motif, 1969.

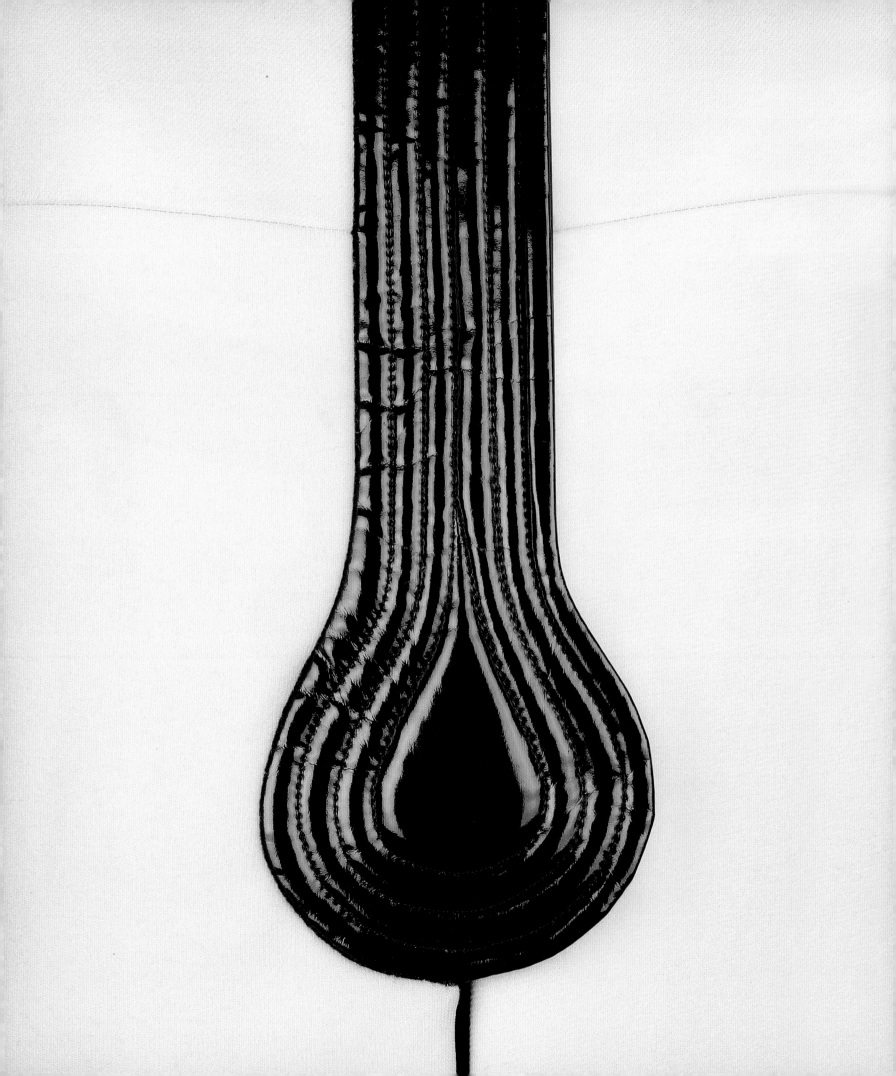

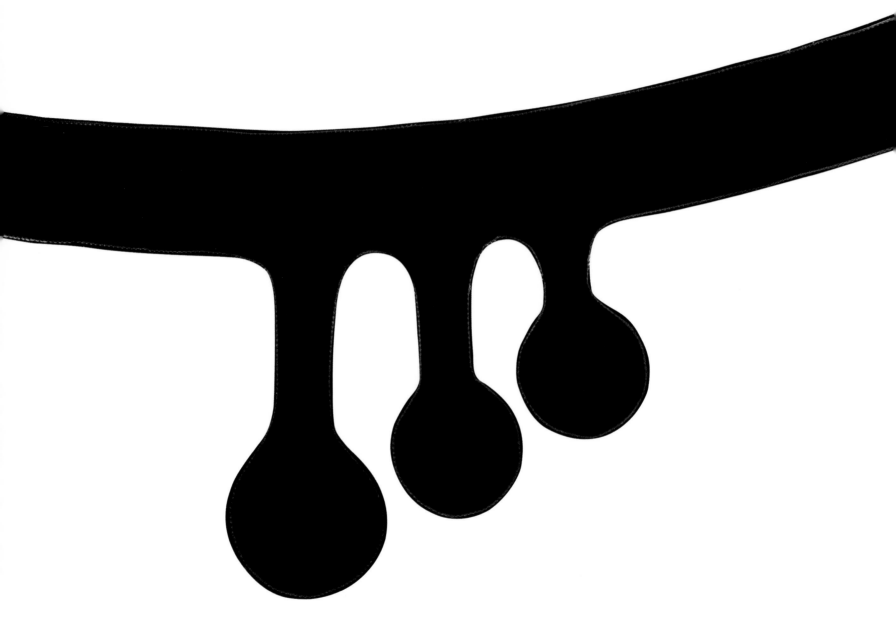

Details of necklaces made of black vinyl and resin, 1970.

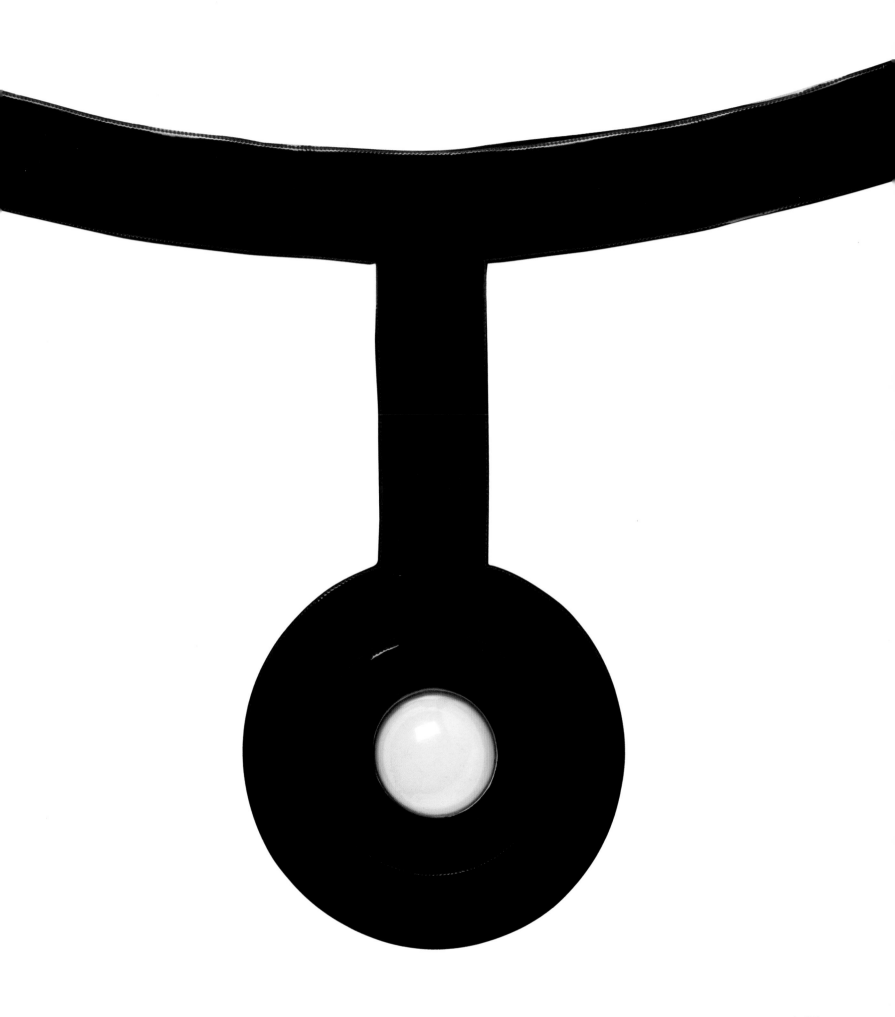

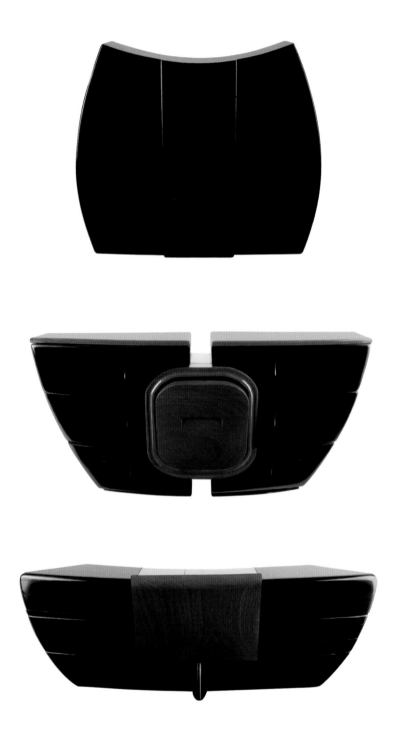

ABOVE AND FACING PAGE Wooden models of storage units that were never produced. Top: storage unit 22" x 18" x 6"; center: cupboard 16" x 8" x 5"; below: bar unit 18" x 6" x 7", circa 1978; Satellite lamp by Yonel Lebovici produced in one hundred copies exclusively for Pierre Cardin, made of three Plexiglas rings around a sphere containing the bulb, mounted on a metal base, 16" x 5" x 16", 1969.

Girafe chair by Serge Manzon in silver-plated
metal, varnished wood and beige lacquered legs,
16" x 31" x 67", 1976–77.

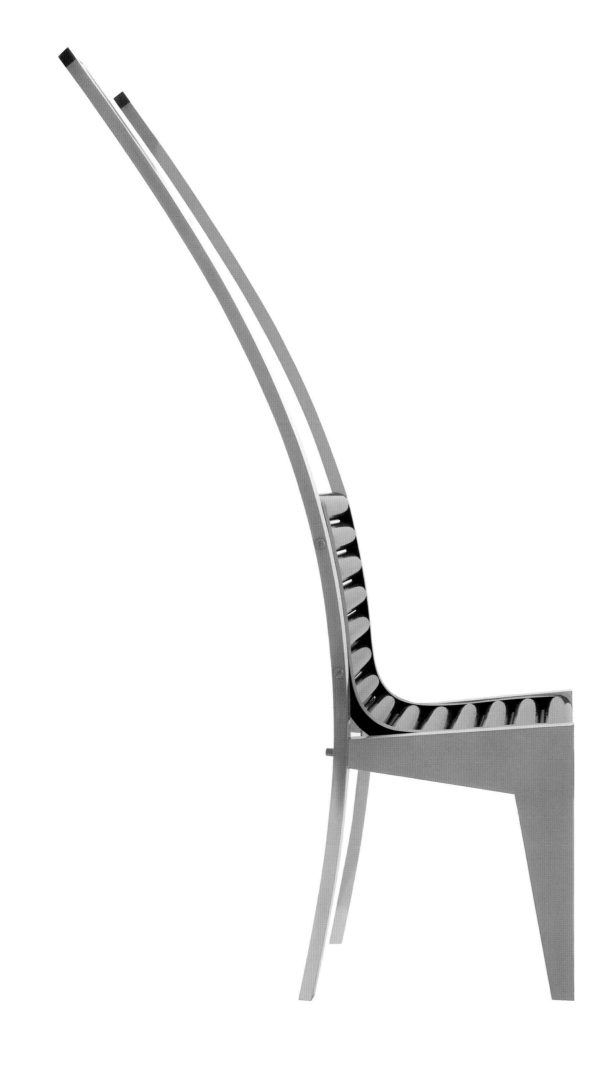

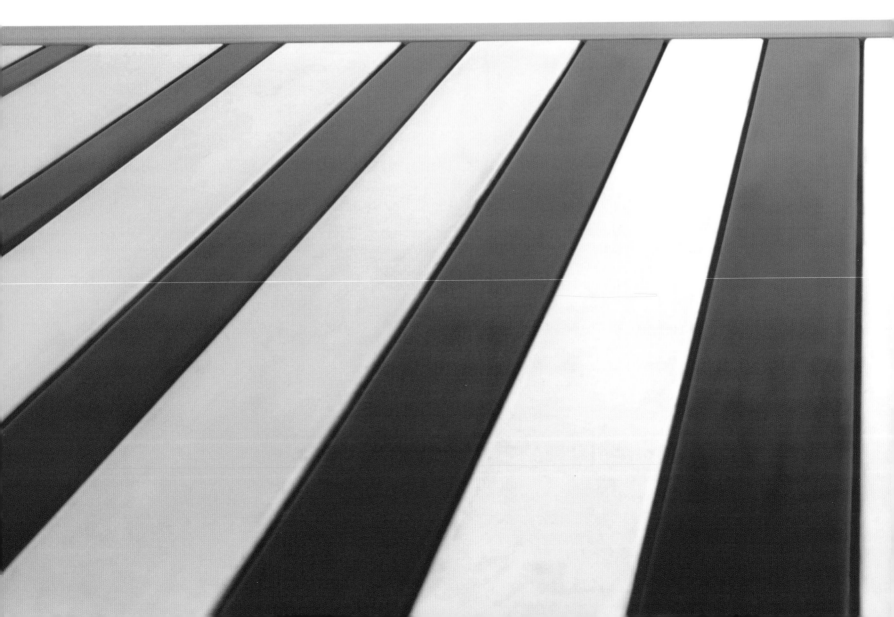

Conference table by Serge Manzon in beige and metallic silver lacquered wood,
composed of veneered strips, 102" x 33" x 30", 1976–77. Detail.

Conference table by Serge Manzon in beige and metallic silver lacquered wood, composed of veneered strips, 102" x 33" x 30", 1976–77.

Dressing table by Serge Manzon in two-tone metal, with a circular mirror
capped with a reflector, fitted with a bulb, 69" x 21" x 62", 1978.

FACING PAGE AND BELOW Large Balance lamp by Serge Manzon composed of an articulated lamp, chrome-plated metal tubular structure, and lit by two bulbs, 39" x 10" x 79", circa 1977; Balance lamp by Serge Manzon, tubular structure in brushed metal, black lacquer cubic tips, brushed metal split reflector, fitted with two bulbs, 24" x 10" x 33", circa 1977.

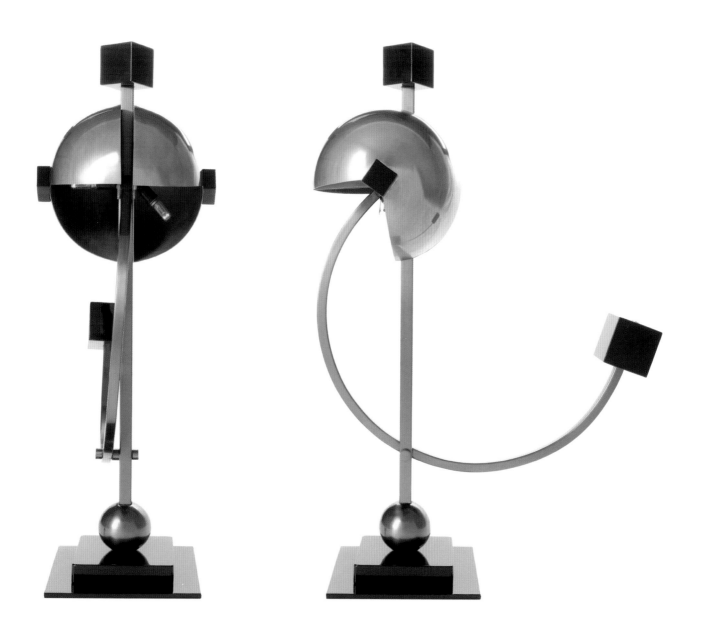

Éclair lamp by Serge Manzon with a brushed metal reflector fitted with a bulb, lacquered brown or blue triangular support and quarter-sphere metallic base, 14" x 9" x 17", circa 1978.

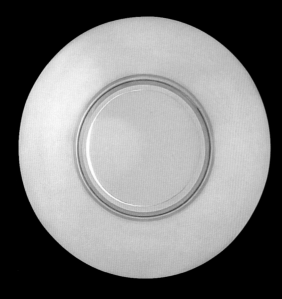

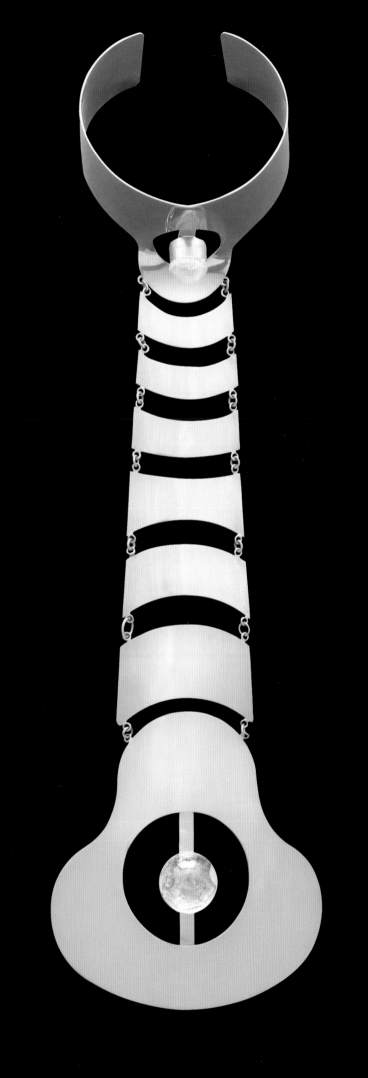

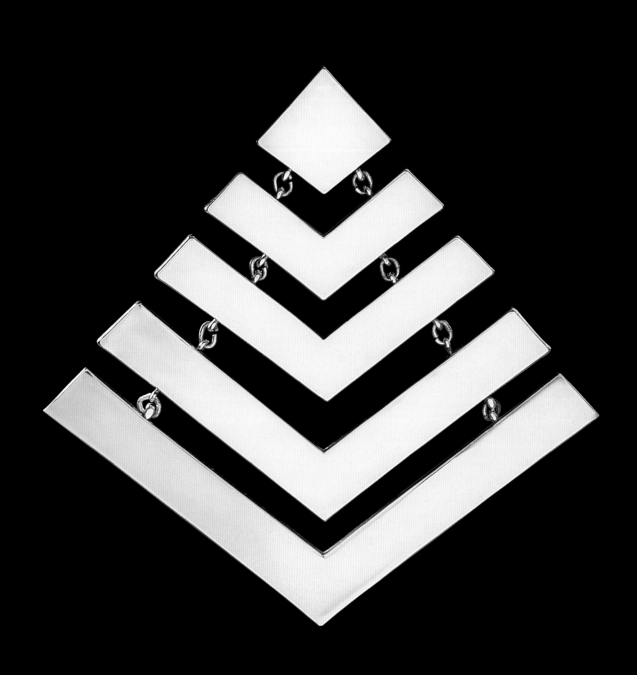

ABOVE AND FACING PAGE Sunglasses in brushed steel, 6" x 4", 1975;
Wallpaper design, Pierre Cardin Design Studio, 1970–75.

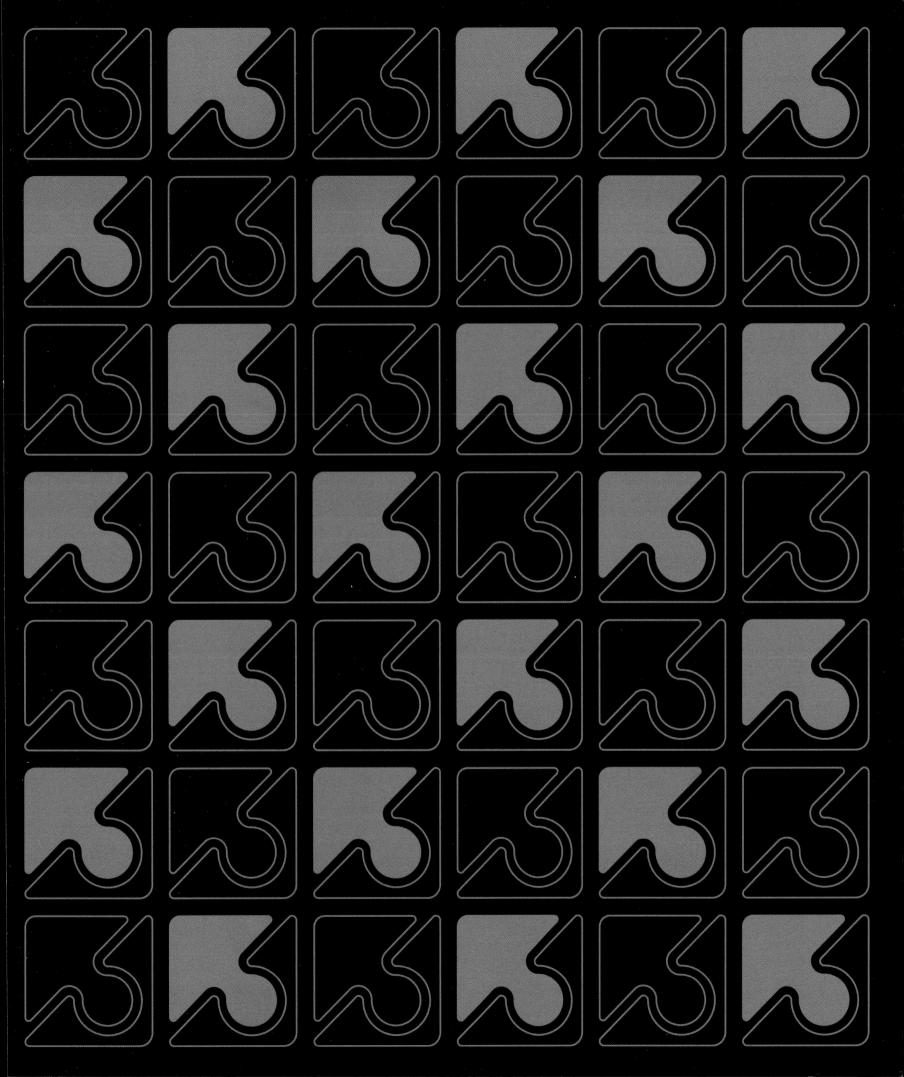

Modular shelving by Christian Adam in two-toned gray lacquered wood,
stacked sections with doors, 104" x 23" x 81", 1977.

Woolen Souches armchairs by Claude Prevost in assorted colors,
59" x 45" x 55", 1977. Detail.

Editions
and licenses

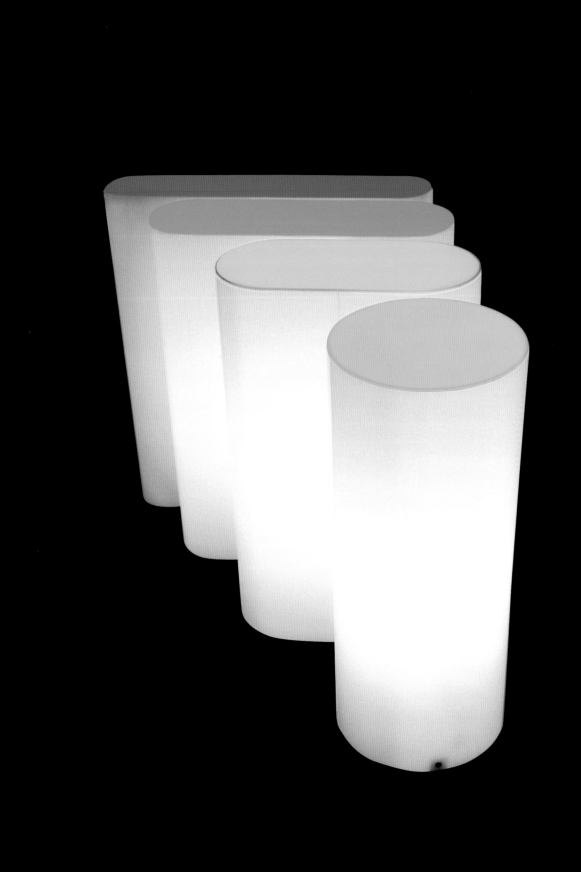

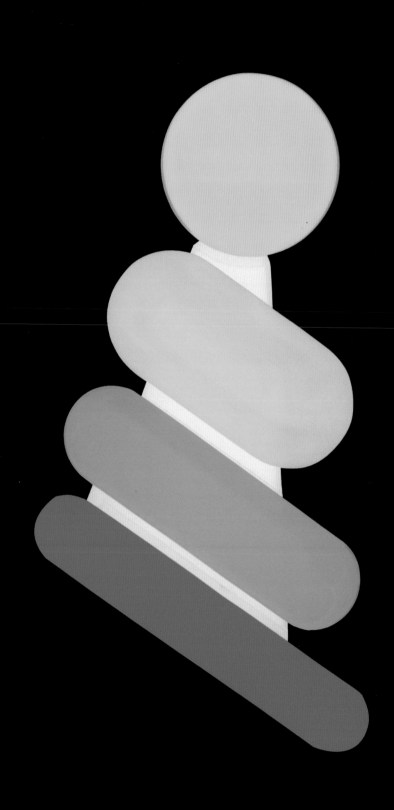

PAGE 175 Pierre Cardin and his West Wind executive jet, 1978.
PRECEDING DOUBLE PAGE Lamps designed by the Pierre Cardin Design Studio and produced
for the Japanese market by Yamada Shomei, 17" x 19" x 23", 1970.
ABOVE AND FACING PAGE Lamps designed by the Pierre Cardin Design Studio and produced
for the Japanese market by Yamada Shomei, 15" x 9" x 30", 1970.

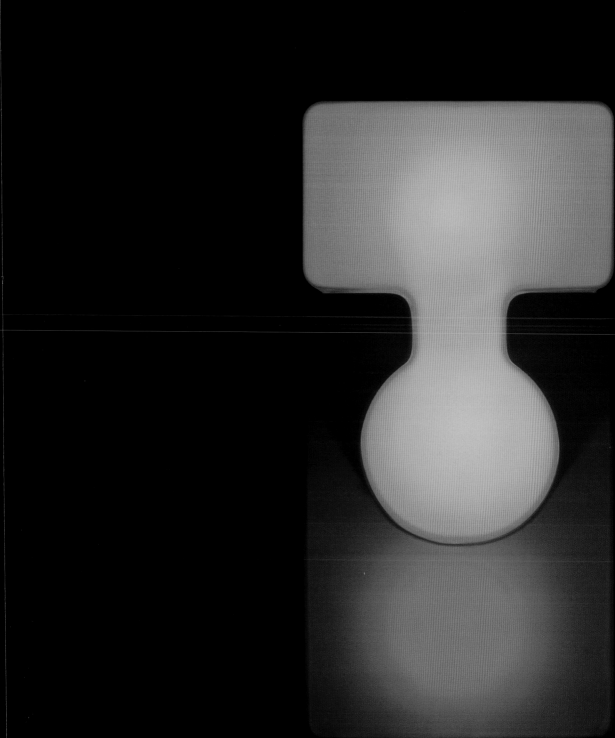

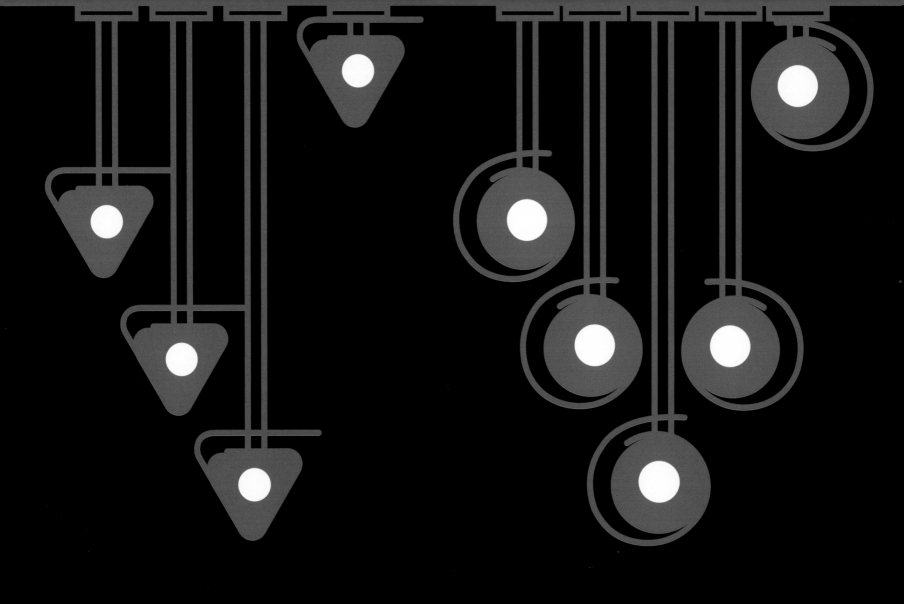

Drawings for a series of lamps designed by the Pierre Cardin Design Studio
and produced for the Japanese market by Yamada Shomei, 1970.

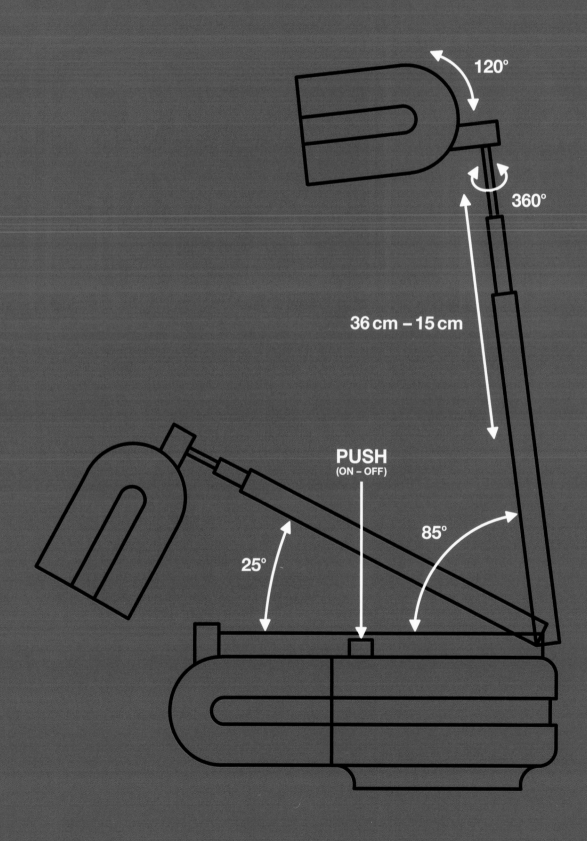

120°

360°

36 cm – 15 cm

PUSH
(ON – OFF)

85°

25°

Maxim armchair designed by the Pierre Cardin Design Studio and produced
by Steiner; metal base and cover in black Larzac angora produced by Placide Joliet,
edged with contrasting colored piping, 39" x 31" x 34", 1978–79.

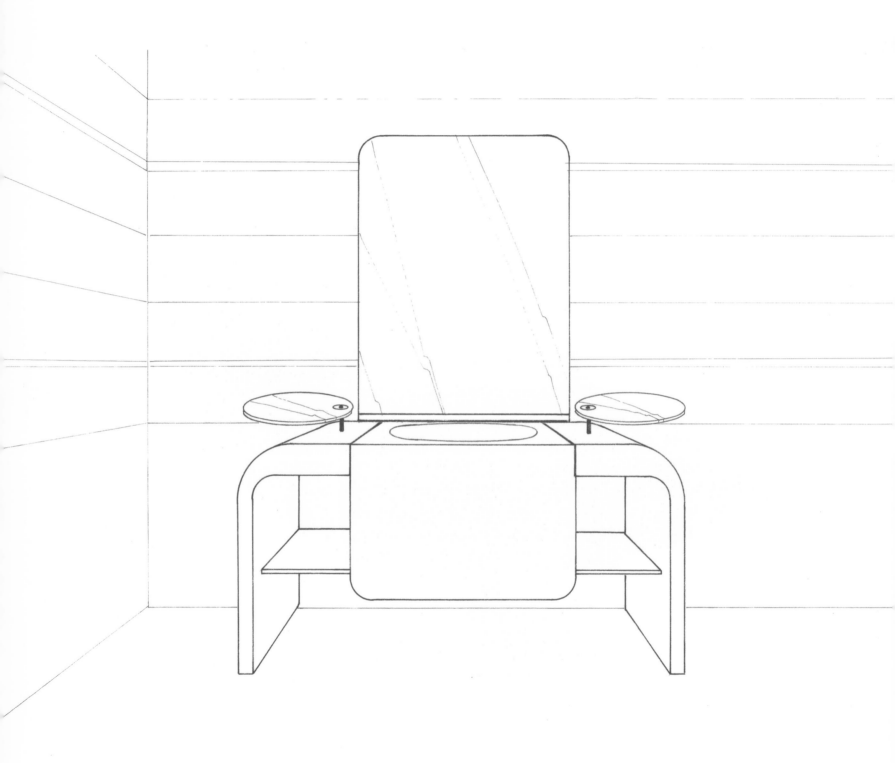

ABOVE AND FACING PAGE Sketch for a bathroom sink, created by the Pierre Cardin design studio, circa 1980; Design for a tap fitting, inspired by the Bleu Marine perfume bottle, circa 1980.

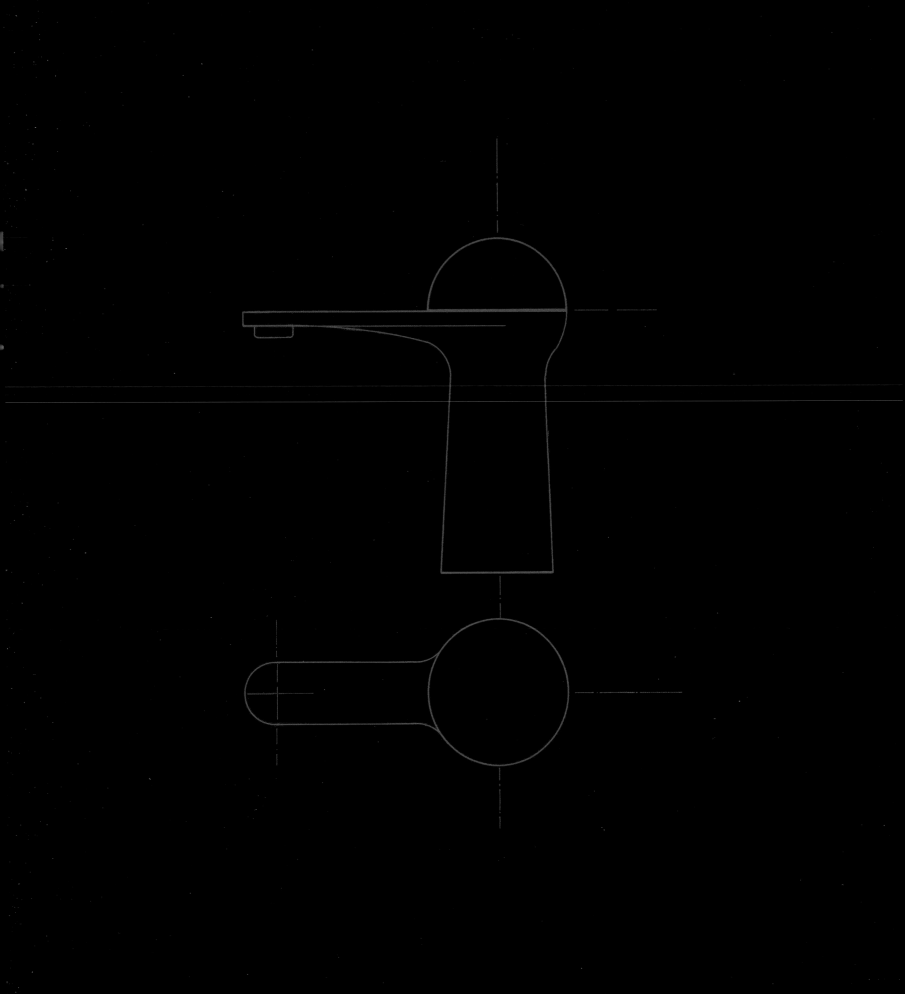

Lic Ato

made in France

FACING PAGE AND ABOVE Table clocks, blue model 5" x 4" x 5"; white model 5" x 4" x 6", 1970. FOLLOWING DOUBLE PAGE, LEFT Wristwatch, movement by Jaeger-LeCoultre, watch-face 2" x 1", bracelet 8" x 1", 1970. RIGHT Wristwatch, movement by Jaeger-LeCoultre, watch-face 1" x 2", bracelet 9" x 1", 1970; Wristwatch, movement by Jaeger-LeCoultre, watch-face 2" x 2", bracelet 8" x 1", 1970.

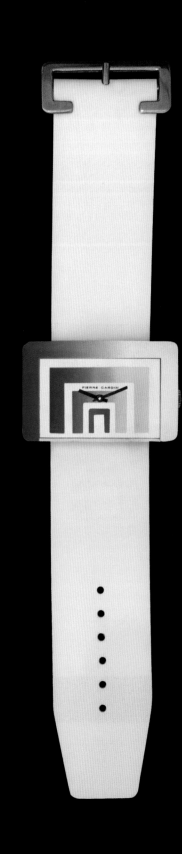

Painted porcelain plates produced by Lafarge, 24.5" diam., circa 1970.

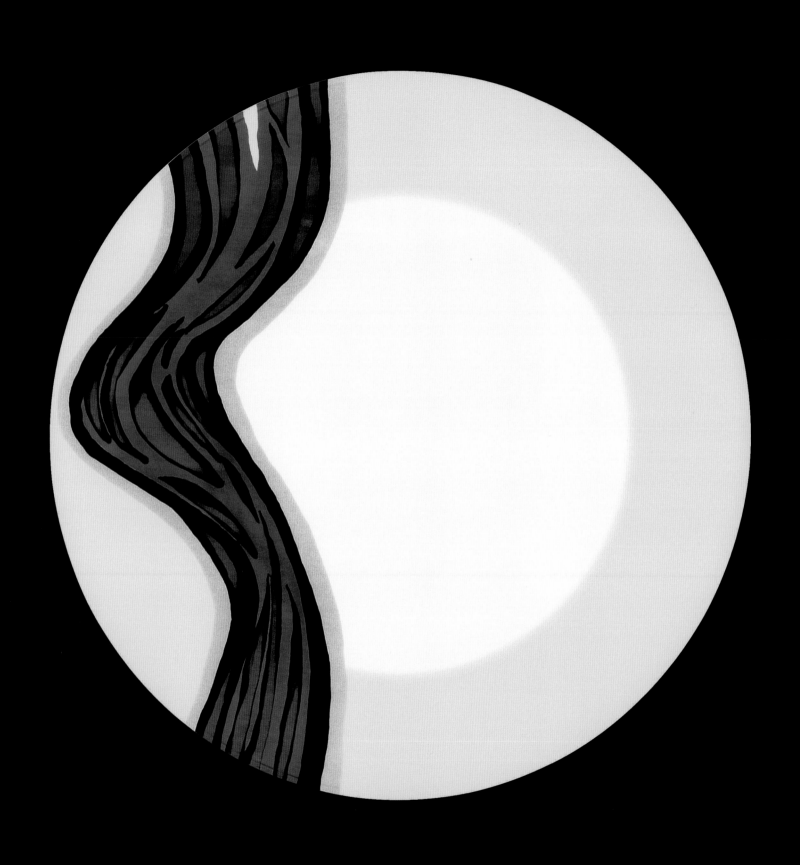

ABOVE AND FACING PAGE Japanese-license lighters, 4" x 4" x 4", 1979;
Japanese-license glass, 3" diam., H. 5", 1979.

The Palais Bulles

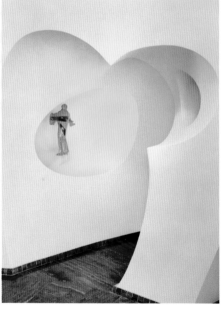

Facing the Bay of Cannes, on the heights of L'Esterel, Pierre Cardin's villa resembles a living organism, a futuristic polypore clinging to the coastline. It blends seamlessly into the Pointe de l'Esquillon vegetation creating a movie dreamscape inhabited by the likes of James Bond girl Ursula Andress lazing languidly at the edge of a crystal blue pool.

The Palais Bulles (or "bubble palace") is one of the many prestigious houses of the Côte d'Azur and South of France, including the Éphrussi villa and Niemeyer's Brasilia villa in Saint-Jean-Cap-Ferrat, the Kerylos villa in Beaulieu, and Eileen Gray's E1027 in Roquebrune-Cap-Martin. Construction commenced in 1975, and was finally completed in 1989. No sooner finished, Pierre Cardin moved in, investing his cellular terracotta-toned lunar yurt with collections of Seventies artwork and furniture. The building was the brainchild of Antti Lovag, the now legendary architect and habitation connoisseur, whose first plastic and quasi-scientific experiments were carried out in 1963. In collaboration with architect Jacques Couëlle, Lovag built his first 'intimist landscape house', based on the shape of a nautilus, in the Alpes-Maritimes region.

Antti Lovag was born in Hungary in 1920, several years before the great 1925 International Exhibition of Decorative and Industrial Arts in Paris, where some of the 20th-century's greatest architects erected groundbreaking, modern pavilions. Fifty years later, the agitator Lovag's own architectural ideal found its expression in this two-acre troglodyte palace where futuristic genius met cave mythology. A 3,937 sq. ft. central vessel of living space, composed of ten rooms devoid of right angles, is surrounded by a tropical garden, swimming pool and 500-seat amphitheatre. In this architectural matrix, furniture and walls blend; only the "Skydome" skylights, spatial windows, eyeglass doors and oval intrusions of the warped, concave or convex walls are sanctioned, soothing curves to smooth the senses. It is as if Antti Lovag has given shape to surrealist artist Tristan Tzara's dream devoid of an intra-uterine architecture (*Minotaure*, 1933). There is something of André Bloc's cabins from 1962, or the Womb House created in Van Lieshout's workshop in 2003: the Palais Bulles rouses the curiosity of the sleeping child within us all. ■

ABOVE, FROM TOP TO BOTTOM Translucent "Skydomes" decorate the ovoid walls, creating an impression reminiscent of *Logan's Run* and other sci-fi movies of the 1970s. In the hollows of the wall, among the giant oogonia, are hidden lamps and other features. In the ovolo, is a sculpture by artist Dario Villalba. **FACING PAGE** The interpenetration of interior and exterior creates orifice-windows and artery-corridors always open to the exterior. **PAGES 196–97** The bay window of the lounge opens onto a spacious, aquatic world: sky, sea and swimming pool blend to create a unified landscape. **PAGES 198–99** Artificial light enhances the cellular forms of the architecture at twilight. **PAGES 200–01** In one of the Palace rooms, two Ovni armchairs by Claude Prevost sprawl in the space age environment.

Interview with Marc Newson
Benjamin Loyauté

You were fifteen in 1978. What do the 1970s represent for you?

The 1970s are of course linked with my childhood, where I lived, the experiences I had and the way I assimilated it all at this period of my life. The 1960s also have an important role in my work, but I should say that the 1970s affected me more in that I was more aware, more mature. I could understand what was happening around me and what I saw in magazines or on television. It was quite a period of Utopia for me. People used bright colors, things were not extravagant, but objects and furniture were interesting, less ordinary. It was easy to notice all this at the time. Now, with hindsight, I can't say that I liked the 1970s because of the particular shapes, colors, plastics, etc. that were used, but because the spirit of those years made a definite impression on the adolescent that I was.

If I was a teenager today I suppose I would be particularly sensitive to what goes on around me. But because I was a teenager in the 1970s, I soaked up the music and films of the period like a sponge. Basically, our naivety makes us permeable to all sorts of influences. I was in Australia at the time, which is interesting because it was a country still isolated from the creative effervescence that was gripping cities like New York, London and Paris. So I had to make a determined effort to understand what was going on elsewhere.

The Seventies are, today more than ever, enjoying a fashion revival. How do you explain the endurance of this particular decade?

I suppose it is because it was a very bold decade, people were not afraid to use certain colors, to look for new means of artistic expression. Today's world is not really joyous; at least I don't think it is. There is more cynicism. The 1970s were lighter. This might sound naïve, but in some ways there is an element of candor in all of my work that is not particularly intentional. This naivety comes from my childhood, because the spirit of the 1970s had something childlike about it.

In one of your books are anamorphic images of the neo-Louis XVI salon from the film *2001: A Space Odyssey* on 3D Orgone Chairs and Felt Chairs. Stanley Kubrick's 1968 film seems to have inspired you. Why?

That's very odd: you must be the first to have noticed. It was initially just a veiled reference, then, later, a true expression of the memory of images. I didn't think that anyone would notice. In this strange white room, nothing motivates the spectator to be attentive. So you need to know how to look, how to dissect. The film sent shivers down my spine. It is a very strong film which appeals to the memory and is at the same time intangible. In the same register, though, I think I prefer the film *Solaris*, which is less graphic and more intellectual.

You are a designer, you design streetwear, so what do you think of couturiers or fashion designers who, like Pierre Cardin in the past or Rick Owens today, start making furniture?

I think it's important. I have always thought it was important for me to be open to other fields such as fashion, music, cinema and suchlike. I think it's the same for other furniture designers, architects, musicians . . . . For me it is important to be interested in, or at least be open to, other fields of contemporary research. This openness influences me enormously. I like to know what is going on around me, especially architecturally. As for my attitude to clothing, it is purely visual. I try to be logical in all my projects. I wear clothes, so I give myself the chance to design what I wear. But this doesn't make me a fashion designer or a couturier. I make no claims on this title. I am simply experimenting in a creative field via clothes, much as I have already tackled cars and watches . . . . it's just another form of expression, another way I can express myself.

Do you think there's an intersection between fashion and design?

Fashion is very difficult. For me there is an obvious relationship between fashion and design. Just as some fashion stylists try their hand at furniture, with varying degrees of success, I am doing the same in reverse. In fact I jump from one discipline to the other. Maybe because I don't want to be pigeonholed into any category, though many designers are. I suppose it's inevitable at some point in your career. History insists on categorizing you. With Pierre Cardin, everything seems to interconnect and work together in a modular way. He is one of the rare people who are able to "jump" from furniture to fashion; he may even be the only one that cannot be labeled with a single skill.

How do you approach the fashion/design relationship in your work?

I personally create clothes to satisfy a desire. My motivation came from the fact that I have to buy myself clothes and I couldn't find anything I liked. It was very frustrating, so I designed my own jackets with graphic prints . . . But when I first started to create my own clothes, I felt a certain amount of resentment towards the fashion world. In the design world, my world, there was a kind of cynicism towards fashion. It's odd, because it's as if, when you cross over into fashion, or when fashion crosses into furniture, it worries a lot of people. Even though there are no major problems involved. If I design buildings or a car or a boat, it is because from a technical point of view I want to do it. In fashion, things move fast, everything is seasonal; the creative process is really interesting. It is a vast experimentation ground. Fashion is so fleeting that it is inconceivable

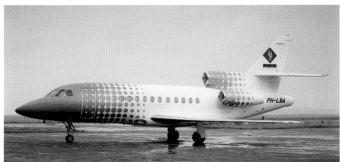

for me. This is one of the reasons that led me to have some fun with clothes, because my work is fundamentally slow. In design and in architecture, it takes two or three years for me to see the final result of a project.

Do you think that a designer should, like a couturier, compose each piece according to the morphology of the human body?

That depends, but it is obvious that a chair has to relate to the human body. There is always a connection with the body. You know, I was trained in jewelry, a field in direct relationship with the body. When I was studying jewelry, I was making furniture, and one day my teacher asked me why. For me it was obvious. A piece of jewelry is connected to the body in the same way as a dress is made for the body. It is always exciting to imagine going beyond various limits. I think that if you can't do this as an industrial designer, you really aren't a very good designer. Pierre Cardin was the first to do it and for that his work deserves to be looked at as you are doing now. You know, people ask how you can design a watch, a plane, a pair of shoes . . . but I think you should be able to apply the same logic and the same language to lots of different things. Technically, these things are the same. The challenge is more or less the same.

The notions of pleasure and sensuality seem to have significant roles in your work. As the "smooth" esthetic was above all representative of speed in the 1960s and 1970s, would you agree that you have since introduced a more carnal element, as your Orgone chair leads us to believe?

Maybe. I can honestly say that if this is visible in my work, it is not deliberate. When I design a piece of furniture, I am not trying to make something sensual. But I can understand my interest for Wilhelm Reich and the Orgone box[1]. If my furniture procures the same kind of compulsion, then . . . . However, I am not exactly sure how this manifests itself or how I have manifested it. I suppose it's an extremely involuntary expression. It comes naturally and it is difficult to isolate the source. Also, having to do tactile things is not a leitmotiv for me. I am simply interested in the material, the process, the technology. Obviously, I am interested in the sensual aspects of design, but for me the way I do things leads to the result that you see. What you say is true; I create furniture like a couturier creates a dress. I always enjoy making things with my hands. I physically created all my first pieces and I still love doing it.

One-off pieces and mass production were Pierre Cardin's leitmotiv. These two creative fields, often considered to be contradictory, are also the subject of your work. How do you think these two approaches are connected?

I do indeed work in these two fields and I think it is for historical reasons. When I was starting out as a designer, I was making one-off pieces or maybe two or three of the same piece. For me, it was the only way to create something. I was in Australia where there were very few factories, so I couldn't count on them to do anything for me. It was obvious that no large company was going to take the risk of producing my creations. I was unknown; no one would have done it. It was impossible to go and see a furniture company and ask them to make something. In fact I think that there were no furniture manufacturers; and if there had been, they would have refused. The only way was to make pieces myself. Making one-off pieces enabled me to be visible, to present my designs to companies, and to the world, in a way. At that time I was of the Opinion that a successful designer should have his pieces mass produced, so that became my dream: to create furniture that would be mass-produced. Unfortunately things turned out differently. My first pieces lived out their existence without ever being manufactured. When I look back at what I have done until now, I can say that even though I have devoted myself to mass production since those early days, I have always understood that the way I worked then was actually very efficient in terms of communication. I get the feeling that this approach is far more effective. The reality is that a one-off piece conveys an image, a reputation that is much more important than any mass-produced piece. So now I try to do both in parallel. The older I get, the better I understand that no one can tell you how to design one-off pieces, the amount they are supposed to be worth, or how to market them. All the decisions concerning my one-off pieces are 100% my responsibility, whereas for mass production, there is a whole chain of people involved in the manufacturing process.

Today, a large part of my work is with the aviation industry, which is very strict. A lot like the firearms industry. Here, the system is different again. It's a real challenge because the creative possibilities are very limited. A certain amount of discipline is required. 60% of what I am doing today is devoted to the new plane, the A380 . . . you can't get much further from a one-off piece than that! But it brings a balance to my working life. Both areas of my work have a healthy existence and despite the fact that they are unconnected, one can influence the other. Yet in terms of the complete process, they are entirely distinct. One day I met David Hamilton, the British artist, and what was fascinating for me was that he also designed computers. So although Pierre Cardin is in people's minds a couturier, your book will at last reveal other important aspects of his identity.

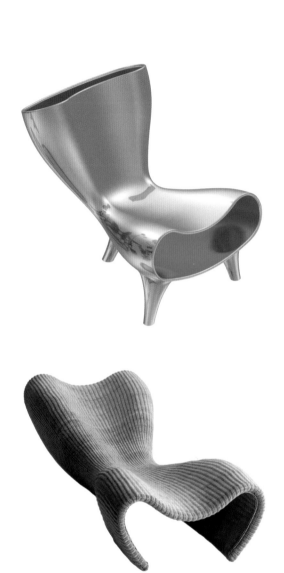

Just as history made Art Deco and its one-off pieces star museum attractions, such as André Groult's anthropomorphic piece that you reinvented, or the Curule chair by Pierre Legrain designed for the couturier Jacques Doucet, your furniture is entering collections at major world museums such as the MoMA in New York with the same vigor. Do you think there exists a culture of one-off pieces and do you think that they have the same aura as a work of art?

I think it's a real and developing phenomenon. All over the world, there is a huge trend for one-off pieces. At the moment, at the Miami Art Fair, everyone was talking about the phenomenon. In September this year (2006), I will have an exhibition at Larry Gagosian's in New York, which is a major gallery that is also beginning to understand the point of this unique "thing". This interest has most probably existed for much longer, I don't know. But what I am sure of is that the contemporary art world is showing more and more interest in designers, offering them exhibitions.

Like Pierre Cardin, you have total control over your materials, to the point where your finished furniture resembles your sketches exactly. At a time when new materials such as Corian are being widely used in "new generation" furniture, have materials always been an obsession of yours, as a kind of guarantee of esthetic success?

I think it goes beyond the materials. They have an essential role to play, but for me they are more a means of expression. People often ask me which is my favorite material, and of course I don't have a favorite. They are the means to an end. Materials to me are like words for a writer: we have to use a lot of words to express ourselves. I am not interested solely in materials; in fact in a way I am obsessed by the process, the techniques and the transformation of materials, the way things are created as much as the materials themselves. Two things really interest me: materials and processes. I don't design in order to collect the objects I create; I don't have a design museum genre. The only thing I get out of designing is knowledge, know-how, and the fact of understanding how to design something new. So I have learnt something. Each time I create an object, it's as if I learn a new lesson, pass a new university diploma.

Design today is impregnated with numerous historical and traditional references. Do you think we need to look back to move forward?

I think we have more opportunities to work on the details. What I mean is that for example if you look at car designers, you notice that they are constantly trying to find the means to reinvent the car. But they still respect the basic idea of the car. It is inherent in their specialty. These designers were born with the conventional notions of a car. When I designed my car, I did the same. I like the car's

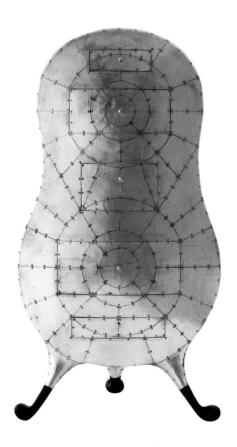

FACING PAGE, FROM TOP TO BOTTOM AND ABOVE Orgone Chair for Pod, 1993; Wicker Lounge for Idée, 1990; Embryo Chair for Idée, 1988; Pod of drawers for Pod, 1987.

conventions. If you look at the car I designed, you will see that it has four wheels. If you ask a child to draw a car, they do the same. My intention is to use this familiarity as a way to help people see beyond conventional ideas. You need to think of all the other little things, the small details, so that the conventional ideas of a car become a kind of framework, a canvas on which you can work. This is why there are reminders in everything that I do. It's completely intentional. If we have a feeling of familiarity or if we think an object is familiar, then I can begin to communicate other ideas. A chair will always be a chair. This is exactly what I have done with furniture. Using a chair as an instrument to express another idea isn't easy. You need to be able to see beyond it. To do so, you need to provide help, an easy, subliminal way for people to make contact with or to react to something when they don't even know how it is made. They understand in a way that there is a reference in their consciousness that has been there for a long time. As you have said, the user shelters under a shared past, shared rules that the designer must be aware of in order to invent the "new". But I always ask, "What is really new?" Sometimes, I think that in one sense, only technology is new. Any object that can be mistaken for a piece of lambda furniture must fight to be completely new. This is not necessarily my aim. My dream is to design and create objects that people like and that provoke a reaction.

What do you think of Pierre Cardin today?

Pierre Cardin was highly influential in both Japan and Australia. He is a man who has always been part of my designer's landscape. I think he was a major forward-looking figure. Unlike Mr. Cardin, I don't have a particular vision of the future; I mean I don't imagine the future having any specific form. I think this is probably because I am working at this precise moment in time. What I do is day-to-day, year-to-year. It isn't all last minute: I do have a few long-term plans. But at the same time I am always thinking about the future, about how to make things that would be in some way appropriate to the future. I try to picture the design of an object and then imagine that object in ten years' time. What will it look like? How will it fit into the world in ten years? Of course you also need to imagine how the world will be in ten years, but I am not obsessed by the future, by the idea of the future. For me the future means new parameters, for example, I see myself able to continue doing what I do now, but with my own conditions attached. Actually, I think I'm already working under my own conditions, so I am already in the future, professionally speaking. What the future might bring for me is perhaps this possibility you mention of creating a kind of empire. I suppose that it is a different future from the one I imagine. I think more about where I will be living,

Glasses, Iittala, 1998.

FROM TOP TO BOTTOM Black Hole Table for Idée, 1988, Mini Event Horizon Table for Cappellini, 1993.

where I want to go, what kind of experiences I want to have. I think more about lifestyle questions than design questions in fact.

How would you define yourself: as a designer or a company? Do you think we will see a Newson empire sometime in the future?

I do of course think about creating an empire, but I suppose unlike Pierre Cardin I can benefit from the fact that he has already done it. In fact, several people have done it; you could even say that Starck has done it too. So unlike Pierre Cardin, who was the first, I am creating my empire on a smaller scale. His is a historical example, I still wonder if it's a good idea, whether I ought to be working towards it or not. At the same time I realize that the most important thing for me is to be able to draw, to design things, to create, because that is really what I love doing. Running a company isn't really my thing; personally, it's my idea of hell. But in order to have the permanent opportunity to design and create things, a minimum of organization is necessary. In some ways, this hatred of companies prevents my organization from being transformed into an "empire". However I could change my mind at any time . . . .

Identity plays a major role in the communication process. Pierre Cardin used his name like a logo, a label: what do you think of this approach?

It is indeed highly distinctive. Of all designers, he is certainly the one about whose work I was never cynical; I have enormous respect for him. Of course it isn't easy to do what he did, in fact it's very difficult. You know, it is so easy to criticize someone; you could find a million reasons to criticize. What you say is true, he thinks about every single thing he does. That is him entirely, it is instantly recognizable; all of his creations are closely linked to his personality. He was the first to do that, to exploit this idea of a logo. Time turns and retraces its steps. The time has now come for everyone to rediscover Pierre Cardin. ■

[1] From the very beginning of his career, Wilhelm Reich was interested in sexuality and particularly the orgasm. His research brought him to the following conclusion: at the moment of orgasm a very specific type of energy is released, energy he called "orgone". But for Reich, far from being confined to sexual pleasure alone, this energy is essential to all aspects of a healthy life. It alone can release man from anxiety and lead him to happiness. However, for certain reasons linked to childhood, the natural orgasmic function is repressed in many people, causing pathological phenomena on both physiological and psychological levels. In 1927, Reich suggested some daring hypotheses in *Genitality in the Theory and Therapy of Neurosis*. This work, and other writings, led to an eventual break with the Freudian school.

Bibliography

General works

Alberto BASSI, Raimonda RICCINI and Cecilia COLOMBO. 2004. *Design in Triennale 1947-1968 percosi fra Milano e Brianza*. Milan: Silvana Editoriale.

Laurence BENAÏM. 2004. *Pierre Cardin, photos de Yoshi Takada*. Milan: Carla Sozanni.

Anne BONY. 2005. *Meubles et décors des années 70*. Paris: Éditions du Regard.

Jean BOSSARD and Anne PIONTKOVSKY, preface by Pierre Cardin. 1970. "Formes industrielles, l'esthétique et le produit." *Les Cahiers I.D.E.E 2*. O.B.M collection, Dunod.

Philippe DECELLE, Diane HENNEBERT, Pierre LOZE. 1994. *L'Utopie du tout plastique 1960-1973*. Brussels: Fondation pour l'architecture. Paris: Norma.

Madeleine DELPIERRE. 1977. *Élégance et création 1945-1975*. Paris: Musée de la mode et du costume.

Dorfles GILLO. 1974. *Introduction à l'industrie design, langage et histoire de la production en série*. Paris: Casterman, Synthèses contemporaines collection.

Ali HANAN and Kate DWYER. 2003. *Intérieurs d'exception, glamour contemporain*. Paris: Octopus.

Anna VENINI DIAZ DE SANTILLANA. 2000. *Venini glass, 1921-1986, catalogue raisonné*. Paris, Skira.

Élizabeth LANGLE. 2005. *Pierre Cardin: Fifty years of Fashion and Design*. London: Thames and Hudson.

Jean MANUSARDI. 1986. *Dix ans avec Pierre Cardin*. Paris: Fanval.

Davide MOSCONI. 1970. *Design Italia 70*. Milan: A. Mauri.

Exhibition catalogues

Benjamin LOYAUTÉ. 2005. *Pierre Cardin evolution design. Espace Pierre Cardin Saint-Ouen, mai 2005*. Paris: Pierre Cardin Éditeur.

Delphine and Yorane LEBOVICI. 2003. *Yonel Lebovici 1937-1998*. Paris: YP Art Expo, 15 square Vergennes.

Sotherby's sales catalogue. 1998. *The Pierre Cardin collection: 21 October 1998*. London: Sotherby's.

Palais des Beaux-Arts, Brussels. 1996. *Mode and Art 1960-1990, palais des Beaux-Arts de Bruxelles, 25 septembre 1995-janvier 1996*. Brussels, Société des expositions du palais des Beaux-Arts.

Valérie MENDES. 1990. *Pierre Cardin: Past, Present, Future. 10 October 1990–6 January 1991*. London: Victoria & Albert Museum. Berlin: Éditions Dirk Nishen.

Jean COURAL, Yolande AMIC, Cécile MIHAILOVIC, Françoise JOLLANT. 1984. *Mobilier national: 20 ans de création, CCI, 29 mai-24 septembre 1984*. Paris: CNACGP.

Immeuble Pierre Cardin. 1983. *Intérieurs 50, apogée de la géométrie curviligne, Immeuble Pierre Cardin*. Brussels: Synergon.

Parinaud ANDRÉ. 1980. *1950–80: European trends in modern art, one hundred paintings, Pierre Cardin Gallery, octobre 1980*. New York.

Danish Foreign Ministry. 1978. *Design danois, Espace Pierre Cardin, 4–14 October 1978*. Paris: Ministère des Affaires étrangères du Danemark.

Espace Pierre Cardin. 1977. "La Couleur dans la ville, 150 sculptures polychromes, Espace Pierre Cardin, 27 mai-30 juin 1977, en partenariat avec le Salon de la jeune sculpture." *Galerie jardin des arts* 170. Paris: Éditions Revues et publications.

Philippe JULLIAN, with texts by Gonzague SAINT-BRIS, Jean-Pierre CAMARD, André CASTELOT, Jacques CREPINEAU, and Yvonne DESLANDRES. 1976. *Sarah Bernhardt, Espace Pierre Cardin, 31 mars-30 mai 1976*. Paris: SIM Éditions.

Espace Pierre Cardin. 1975. *27e Salon de la jeune sculpture, Espace Pierre Cardin and jardin des Champs-Élysées, 9 mai-8 juin 1975*. Paris: Association de la jeune sculpture.

Pierre RESTANY, with texts by Mikis THEODORAKIS, William BURROUGHS, and Allen GINSBERG. 1974. *Les Musicales de Takis, Espace Pierre Cardin, festival d'Automne, octobre 1974*. Paris: Alexandre Iolas Éditeur.

Espace Pierre Cardin. 1974. *Kosice: eau-lumière-mouvement, la cité hydrospatiale, Espace Pierre Cardin, décembre 1974*. Paris: Espace Pierre Cardin.

Pierre RESTANY. 1973. *Dario Villalba, Espace Pierre Cardin, novembre 1973*. Paris: Espace Pierre Cardin.

Espace Pierre Cardin. 1973. *Multiples d'aujourd'hui, Espace Pierre Cardin, cat. de la vente du 17 mai 1973*. Paris: M. C. Tubiana Éditeur.

Espace Pierre Cardin. 1972. *Sculptures et empreintes Krajberg, galerie de l'Espace Pierre Cardin, 11 avril-3 mai 1972*. Paris: Espace Pierre Cardin.

Madeleine GINSBURG. 1971. *Fashion an Anthology by Cecil Beaton, Victoria & Albert Museum, October 1971–January 1972*. London: Victoria & Albert Museum.

Marc GAILLARD. 1970. *Plastiques et art contemporain, Parc des expositions, 2-10 juin 1970*. Paris: Éditions Michel Jankowski.

Monograph articles (selection)

As Pierre Cardin's design activity was essentially concentrated between 1968 and 1983, the 1990s do not figure in this selection.

▪ 1960s

Paris Match, "Pierre Cardin," November 25, 1961.

Paris Match, "Pierre Cardin – Nehru et Jackie Kennedy," March 24, 1962.

Réalités Fémina, "Pierre Cardin," November 1, 1962.

Plaisir de la maison, "Le Jardin d'hiver de Pierre Cardin," October 1, 1964: 30–33.

Life Magazine, "Pierre Cardin," September, 1967.

L'Express, "Les Couturiers refont fortune," February 26–March 3, 1968: 49–54.

Le Figaro, "Cardin relève le défi américain," March 1, 1968.

Play Men 5, "Pierre Cardin," July 1, 1968.

Gérald ASARIA. "Le Pari de Pierre Cardin." *Paris Match*, February 8, 1969.

"Tre per cardin: un nuevo negozio di Pierre Cardin a Parigi." *Domus* 472 (1969): 23–25.

"Pierre Cardin in Milan." *Mobilia* 172 (1969).

"Cardin per la casa." *Domus* 481 (1969).

Courrier de l'Ouest, "Pierre Cardin sort ses griffes," December 22, 1969: 39–40.

▪ 1970s

"Milano, sempre tre per Cardin," *Domus* 483 (1970).

"Pierre Cardin's glass objects by Venini." *Interiors* 129 (1970).

Interior Design, "Maria Pergay, beautiful steel furniture designs," July, 1970.

Geneviève GAILLET. "Cardin à Milan : du cousu main." *Le Figaro*, September 30, 1970.

Odile GRAND. "Cet ensemble signé Cardin." *L'Aurore*, November 16, 1970.

Interior Design, "Market Spotlight," September, 1971.

Interior Design, "Graphiquement – à propos de Pierre Cardin," September, 1971.

Interior Design, "À propos de Pierre Cardin," September, 1971.

Le Figaro, "La Dernière idée flèche de Cardin," September 28, 1971.

Michel DE RÉ. "À l'Espace Pierre Cardin." *Vogue*, November, 1971.

Pierre JOLY and Véra CARDOT. "Exposition Fernand Léger, modernité de la mode : l'Espace Cardin." *L'Œil* 204 (1971.): 34–39.

Pierre JOLY and Véra CARDOT. "Modernité de mode : l'Espace Cardin." *L'Œil* 204 (1971.).

Vogue America, "Your sphere," January, 1972.

"Pacos : place au plastique." *Connaissance des arts* 239 (1972): 50–57.

Anne MANSON and Michel DUNOIS. "Une nuit de folie à l'Espace Cardin." *L'Aurore*, January 26, 1972.

Elle, "Pierre Cardin," February 21, 1972.

Marie Claire, "La Boîte magique de Cardin," March, 1972.

Marie Lavie Compin. "Pierre Cardin dans l'espace." *Vogue*, March, 1972.

"Frans Krajcberg, exposition à l'Espace Pierre Cardin," *L'Œil* 209 (1972): 35.

Newsweek, "Pierre Cardin's Grand Design," July, 1972.

Vogue, "Pierre Cardin, l'innovateur," September, 1972.

"Du marbre dans la nouvelle collection de Pierre Cardin," *Connaissance des arts* 260 (1973).

"Un rêveur professionnel : Serge Manzon," *L'Œil* 219 (1973).

"Bruno Schmeltz, exposition à l'Espace Pierre Cardin," *Connaissance des arts* 264 (1974): 103.

Novum Gerbrauchsgraphik, "Pierre Cardin, Paris/Karl Korab, Wien," April, 1974.

Stefania MANFREDI. "Pierre Cardin." *Casa Amica* 6 (1974): 50–51.

Hoga des Lunes, "Pierre Cardin: creator, hombre de negocios y millonario," October 7, 1974.

Time, "Pierre Cardin," December 23, 1974.

Vogue, "Un deuxième espace," December, 1974–January, 1975.

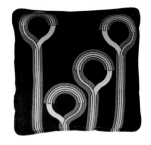

"Pacos/Kosice," *L'Œil* 234/235 (1975): 54.

Réalités, "Le Bon goût c'est nous," March, 1975: 44–48.

Vogue, "Les Favoris," March, 1975: 138–39.

Maïten BOUISSET. "Les Musicales de Takis : Espace Pierre Cardin." *xxᵉ siècle* 44 (1975): 170.

Paris Match, "Pierre Cardin," August 23, 1975.

Roy STUART. "Le Reflet de Pierre Cardin." *L'Œil* 242 (1975): 69–77.

"Le Marché du siège contemporain." Union nationale des Industries françaises de l'ameublement, *Hexaform* 1 (1975): 50–60.

Jours de France, "Pierre Cardin," March 1, 1976.

Architecture intérieure, "La Magie d'une griffe," May–June, 1976.

Courrier du meuble, "Des meubles au laser," April 1, 1977.

Interior Design, "Top Name at High Point," June, 1977.

Courrier du meuble, "La Couleur dans la cité – sculptures et mobilier d'avant-garde," June 24, 1977.

Roseline RUTHER. "La Couleur dans la cité Boris Tabacoff." *Offrir,* September, 1977.

Le Figaro, "Pierre Cardin fait du xviiiᵉ... contemporain," October 20, 1977.

Le Monde, "Jambes croisées dans la tortue," October 22, 1977.

"Altman debuts Pierre Cardin furnishings," *Interiors Design* 48 (1977): 56.

"Mueble de 'Alta costura'," *Cambio 16 Internacional* 315 (1977).

"Pierre Cardin: i mobili-scultura," *Casa Vogue* 77 (1977).

Revue de l'ameublement, "Pierre Cardin et le meuble," December, 1977.

"Évolution ou révolution : les meubles haute couture de Pierre Cardin," *L'Officiel Homme* 5, (1978).

"Dove: una guida agli acquisti," *Casa Vogue* 84/85, (1978).

L'Officiel de l'ameublement, "Contemporain design," January, 1978.

"Paris : Pierre Cardin Évolution," *L'Œil* 270/271 (1978).

Domicible, "Pierre Cardin dans ses meubles," March, 1978.

L'Industria del Legno & del Mobile, "Mobili-scultura di Pierre Cardin," May, 1978.

"Évolution Pierre Cardin," *Domus* 586 (1978).

Bolaffiarte, "Design: le novità," September-October, 1978.

Marie-Pierre DE CICCO, "Les Meubles sculptures utilitaires de Pierre Cardin," *Vogue,* December, 1978–January, 1979.

Maurice RHEIMS. "Les Meubles de Cardin." *La Tribune des arts,* 1979.

La Revue de l'ameublement, "Cardin : collection 79," January, 1979.

C. CHAZELLE. "Pierre Cardin launches furnitures as Art – Pierre Cardin lance le meuble œuvre d'art." *Galerie des arts* 1988 (1979): 74–75 and illustrations: 77.

Raymond BETTY. "Atlantic aviation's Westwind." *Interiors,* February, 1979.

Vogue, "Cardin en Chine," March, 1979.

Susan PATTERSON. "Pierre Cardin, one-man cartel." *Réalités,* March, 1979.

Kimpy BAUMGARTNER. "Espace Pierre Cardin." *L'Œil* 284 (1979): 77.

Aline LONGUET-MONNIER. "Pierre Cardin, meuble ou sculpture ?" *Demeures et châteaux* 4, spring (1979).

QG, "Pierre Cardin: success story," April, 1979.

Madame Figaro, "L'Empereur Cardin règne sur 63 pays," April, 1979.

Susan HELLER-ANDERSON. "Design Dialogue: An interview with Pierre Cardin." *Architectural Diges* 36 (1979): 36.

Le Courrier du meuble, "Sculptures utilitaires de Pierre Cardin," October, 1979.

Vogue, "Dans un monde d'énergie solaire, des vêtements ornements décoratifs des corps libres," November, 1979.

Jours de France, "Chez Pierre Cardin," November 24, 1979.

La Revue de l'ameublement, "Cardin 80," December, 1979.

"Pierre Cardin donne une impulsion contemporaine au meuble français," *L'Officiel de la couture et de la mode* 658 (1979): 226–29.

■ 1980s

Toby Rodes. "Internationale Mobelmesse Koln." *MD* 3 (1980): 28–43.

"Internationale Mobelmesse Koln," *MD* 5 (1980): 40–53.

"Offensichtlich Pierre Cardin," *MD* 4/5/6 (1980): 46–48.

"Cardin Macht Moebel," *MD* 1/2/3 (1980): 55–56.

Jim KEMP. "Une vraie folie (Antti Lovag creates a home recalling lunar landscapes and underseas worlds)." *Residential Interiors,* January, 1980.

MD Moebel Interior Design, "Internationale Mobelmesse Koln 15," January 20, 1980.

Vogue, "Des Tables séductions: table à cœur ouvert de Yonel Lebovici – Pierre Cardin," May, 1980.

William LANSING-PLUMB. "And now... Gloria Vanderbilt bun warners." *Industrial Design US* 4, vol. 27, (1980).

Vogue, "Les Rendez-vous d'octobre, Cardin croit à l'art d'aujourd'hui, sismographie de notre temps," October, 1980.

La Revue de l'ameublement, "Les Meubles de Pierre Cardin au Salon d'Automne," November, 1980.

Réussites, "Bouvard déshabille Cardin," January, 1981.

Interior Design, "Restoration on 57th Street," May, 1981: 287–89.

Elle, "Pierre Cardin," July 20, 1981.

Paris Match, "Pierre Cardin," December 11, 1981.

"Visual Image: Haute Couture Alexandre A," *Novum Gebrauchsgraphik* 4 (1983): 16–21.

CNAC Magazine, "Mobilier national, 20 ans de création," July–August, 1984.

Vogue Homme, "Pierre Cardin," November 1, 1986.

Paris Match, "Pierre Cardin," February 26, 1988.

Claudine FARRUGIA. "Paysage du design industriel." *Intramuros,* July–August, 1988.

Louna, "Pierre Cardin par Paco Rabanne," December 1, 1989.

■ 2000s

Duth ROBIN. "Polka Dots and Moonbeams." *Blueprint* 175 (2000): 84–86 and 88.

Julie STREET. "House of Cardin." *Wallpaper* 32 (2000): 127–28 and 130.

Henrietta THOMPSON. "Gods of all Creation." *New Design* 2 (2001): 58–61.

Bruno DE LAUBADÈRE. "Vive la différence." *Interior Design* (2002): 164–71.

"Antti Lovag: Habitilogue," *Nest* 20 (2003): 92–111.

Benjamin LOYAUTÉ. "Le Bal des Seventies." *AD France,* June, 2005.

Judy FAYARD. "Planet Paris." *Interior Design,* April, 2004.

Patrick FAVARDIN. "Maria Pergay." *Citizen K,* autumn-winter, 2004.

Book collections

LONDON: Victoria and Albert Museum;
NEW YORK: Metropolitan Museum;
PARIS: Bibliothèque des Arts décoratifs, Bibliothèque Forney, Bibliothèque de l'INHA/Fonds Jacques Doucet, Bibliothèque Kandinsky/Centre de documentation et de recherche, Bibliothèque nationale de France, Musée des Arts décoratifs, Musée de la Mode et du Textile, Palais Galliera;
SAINT-OUEN: Musée Pierre-Cardin.

Archives

Michel Blanchon Archives, Francesco Bocola Archives, Cante-Pacos Archives, Pierre Cardin Archives, Gueza Karnay Archives, Denis Laur Archives, Lebovici Archives, Serge Manzon Archives, Giacomo Passera Archives, Maria Pergay Archives, Claude Prevost Archives, Tabacoff Archives.

Other sources

Radioscopie, entretien de Pierre Cardin and Jacques Chancel. Paris: BPI-Bibliothèque du centre Georges-Pompidou.

ABOVE Cushion with woven wool cover, 14" x 14", 1971–72.

Japanese license plastic Thermos flask, large model 6" diam., H. 16";
small model 12" diam., H. 12", 1981.

Index

Numbers in italic refer to illustrations.

Aknowledgements

A work of this nature would never have been possible without the collaboration of those whose experience and memories enabled me to penetrate Pierre Cardin's complex universe, encompassing as it does the worlds of art, fashion, and design. First, I wish to thank Pierre Cardin himself for entrusting this work to me, and Emmanuel Beffy who granted me authorship, without whom the work would never have been produced. I also wish to thank Jean-Louis Gaillemin for his invaluable, never-ending teaching and encouragement, and through him, commemorate the life and work of Philippe Jullian.

Research and documentation for this work could never have taken place without the assistance and efficiency of the ever-present Marie Farman.

I also wish to thank:

Madame Marie-Christine Cardin-Edwards and Eric Edwards,

Pierre Cardin's collaborators who allowed me access to their archives and memories, or their families and friends who keep their work and histories alive: Christian Adam, Christian Baudier, Francesco and Gabriele Bocola, François Cante-Pacos, Elein Fleiss for Serge Manzon, Yorane and Delphine Lebovici, Sophie Majani, Giacomo Passera, Maria Pergay, Yvon Poullain, Claude Prevost, Françoise Moulin-Prevost and Cécile Tabacoff.

The former members of the design studio: Michel Blanchon, Joanna Boillat, Marc Jaricot, Gueza Karnay, Denis Laur, Jean-Marc Lecomte and Lucile Roybier;

The Pierre Cardin establishment: Sergio Altieri, Geneviève Bennequin, Dominique Boitel, Julien Clément, Maryse Gaspard, Antoine Geoffroy d'Assy, Jérôme Faggiano, Jean-Pascal Hesse, Kimiyoshi Miura, Yoshi Takata, Renée Taponier, Richard Raczynski.

The Flammarion team for their marvelous availability and efficiency: Suzanne Tise-Isoré, Bernard Lagacé, Nils Herrmann, Delphine Montagne, Nathalie Chapuis.

All those interested in my research, in particular Marc Newson and Sophie Le Corre.

I also wish to thank: Yves Badetz (Mobilier national), Nicole Bernard, Caroline Berton (*Vogue* archives), Sébastien Cambray-Pellegrin, Claire Chassine, Bertrand Cornette de Saint-Cyr, Nicolas Denis, Nathalie Dumoulin (Kandinsky Library), Patrick Favardin, Jean Paul Gaultier, Matthias Jousse, Christine Jullien (Kandinsky Library), Pascal Juste, François Lafanour, Frédérique Lagache, Michèle Lajournade (Roger-Viollet agency), Dominique and Liliane Loyauté, Diane de Mascarel, Jean-Pierre Piton (Kandinsky Library), Sébastien Sans, Guillaume Savin, Jean-Jacques Wattel, as well as the staff at the national decorative arts library and Bibliothèque Forney, not forgetting those who prefer to remain anonymous.

Photographic Credits

BELOW Énigme perfume, glass flask, 6" x 3" x 1", 1992.
FOLLOWING DOUBLE PAGE Enigme bar unit by Rodrigo in black gloss PMMA and stainless steel. Lighting unit and mobile with ten electric doors, 39" x 17" x 36", 2006.
PAGE 216 Logo designed by Alain Carré for Pierre Cardin, circa 1970–71.

ENIGME
de
pierre cardin

pierre cardin